IMAGES
of America
TURNER STATION

ON THE COVER: Members of Boy Scout Troop 270 are shown in this 1968 photograph with their scoutmaster, James Louden (back row). The troop participated in this annual camping trip at Broad Creek, Maryland, with other units from around the state. Louden was not only a Scout leader for decades but was also active in the local recreation council. (Courtesy of the Louden family.)

IMAGES
of America

TURNER STATION

Jerome Watson
Turner Station Heritage Foundation

ARCADIA
PUBLISHING

Published by Arcadia Publishing
Charleston SC, Chicago IL, Portsmouth NH, San Francisco CA

Library of Congress Catalog Card Number: 2008920965

For all general information contact Arcadia Publishing at:
Telephone 843-853-2070
Fax 843-853-0044
E-mail sales@arcadiapublishing.com
For customer service and orders:
Toll-Free 1-888-313-2665

Visit us on the Internet at www.arcadiapublishing.com

This book is dedicated to all individuals past and present who have contributed to the growth, development, and success of the historic African American community of Turner Station, Maryland.

CONTENTS

ACKNOWLEDGMENTS

I would like to express my sincere thanks and appreciation to everyone who contributed to the success of this book. To all who attended the photograph collection activity at St. Matthews Methodist Church in November, thanks for your interest and participation. To the volunteers from the Baltimore County Public Library, thanks for your support in interviewing, documenting, and scanning numerous images at that event. A special thanks to the following individuals who made substantial contributions to our collection of photographs: Charles and Veronica Mandy, Shirley Bobian Macklin, Rhonda Quarles, Veda Cooper, Olivia Lomax, James Louden, Elsie Winston, Mary Livingston, Dunbar Brooks, Maxine Thompson, and Herbert Harwood.

Jason Domasky of the Baltimore County Public Library (BCPL) provided technical advice and support to our image collection effort. Richard Parsons (BCPL) expedited the reproduction of the many Legacy Web images requested. Jean Walker of the Dundalk–Patapsco Neck Historical Society and Museum gave us access to great photographs of Bragg School. The staff at the News American archives was most helpful in giving us access to its extensive collection of images. Marilyn Benadaret, archivist at the Afro-American Newspapers, also provided assistance with their collection of photographs.

I am indebted to Roland Dorsey of the *Dundalk Eagle*, whose scanning expertise is in full display in this book. Charles Echols Sr. delivered excellent photographs, especially those of the churches. John McGrain, former Baltimore County historian, provided exhaustive detailed documentation of the Turner Passenger Station, giving meaningful insight to the origins of the name Turner Station. Charles Plantholt of the Baltimore Streetcar Museum provided great photographs of the No. 26 streetcars.

I want to thank Cheryl Brooks for her timely assistance with interviews and scanning and Catherine Martin for her excellent work with scanning. I wish to thank Dr. Theodore Patterson, who has been a most valuable resource with his keen insight and critique of this effort. I also thank Lauren Bobier of Arcadia Publishing for gently prodding and keeping this project on track.

Thanks to Courtney Speed, whose tireless commitment and belief in this endeavor are matched only by her hard work and dedication to this community. Finally, thanks to Edie Brooks, whose tenacity and incomparable research skills have again yielded so many gems in photographs and information.

INTRODUCTION

Located on the waterfront in southeast Baltimore County, south of Dundalk and north of the Francis Scott Key Bridge, Turner Station has a rich history with a legacy of achievement. Little is known about the early years. The community had its origins around the late 1800s in an area between Dundalk Avenue and Main Street called the "Meadow," where a small number of families settled. In 1888, a passenger freight station was built by the Baltimore and Sparrows Point Railroad on land belonging to Joshua J. Turner, a local businessman. The train stop came to be known as Turner Station. From its modest beginning in the Meadow, the community grew to the south and east to become the largest black enclave in Baltimore County by 1970.

The early 20th century saw Turner Station emerge from a small settlement to a full-blown community. New residents steadily moved in, prompting the need for services and amenities. Due to racial segregation and the isolation of the community, residents became self-reliant and self-sufficient. During these early years, the Balnew Improvement Association was created to advocate for more infrastructure improvements and black business development. In 1900, the first church, St. Matthews Methodist Church, was founded. It was the first of many congregations to be established in the community. The first public school, Turner Elementary School, opened in 1925 with two portable buildings. In 1930, a new brick facility was constructed at Pine and Chestnut Streets to replace the original structure.

In the area of entertainment, an important establishment came into being in 1933: Adams Bar and Cocktail Lounge. It attracted some of the true icons of the 1930s, 1940s, and 1950s, including comedian Red Foxx, singers Pearl Bailey and Fats Domino, big-band leader Cab Calloway, and other notable entertainers of that era. The Edgewater Beach (1929–1941) was another source of entertainment and recreation. Owned by Dr. Joseph Thomas, it featured a ballpark, a variety of rides, restaurants, a dance hall, and live entertainment.

World War II set the stage for tremendous growth in Turner Station. As the nation prepared for war, demand for steel and steel products created by Bethlehem Steel increased the need for workers and contributed to the community's growth and vitality. General Motors, Western Electric, Continental Can, and other major employers also contributed to the community's growth. Attracted by the employment opportunities, African Americans migrated to the area in great numbers, with many coming from the upper South (Virginia, North Carolina, and South Carolina). Consequently, there was an acute shortage of housing. This led to construction of Ernest Lyon, Day Village, Sollers Homes, Turner Homes, and other housing developments by the federal government and private investors during the 1940s. The increase in population, especially among school-age children, generated demands from parents and community leaders, for much-needed educational facilities. Great strides were made in education with the opening of Fleming Elementary School in 1944 and Sollers Point Junior-Senior High School in 1948. Another by-product of the war was increased demand for services of all types, including entertainment. Dr. Joseph Thomas, the first local physician, built a state-of-the-art, 700-seat, air-conditioned motion picture theater in late 1945. It opened in early 1946 and was named the Anthony Theater after his father.

During the 1950s, the community grew and prospered, as churches, civic and social organizations, recreational activities, and small businesses flourished in response to community needs. The entrepreneurial spirit was evident in the creation of barbershops, beauty salons, grocery stores, gas stations, taxicab companies, trucking firms, television repair shops, and various other businesses. Examples of these businesses were Shelton Cab Company, Acme Market, Jimmy's Barber Shop, Burrell's Five and Dime, Allmond's Grocery Store, Jones Amoco Station, Mondie's Cleaners, and Village Drugstore. Also in the 1950s, three new churches were founded: Greater St. John Baptist Church (1952), Mount Olive Baptist Church (1955), and Christ the King Catholic Church (1956). Last but not least, the Turner Station Recreation Council provided youth with numerous outlets for recreation and social interaction through its programs, which included baseball, basketball, gymnastics, and other activities.

By this time (1950s), Turner Station had evolved into a vibrant, self-sustaining community of over 10,000 residents. Its citizens contributed to the county, state, and nation in a variety of ways. These individuals included Dr. Joseph Thomas (physician, businessman, and diplomat), Kweisi Mfume (Baltimore City councilman, congressman, and NAACP president and chief executive officer), and Calvin Hill (former All-Pro NFL running back for the Dallas Cowboys). Others were Larry Middleton (former top-10-ranked heavyweight boxing contender), Henrietta Lacks (medical science pioneer, whose "HeLa" cells contributed to the creation of the polio vaccine), Kevin Clash (creator of Elmo and nationally known puppeteer), Robert Curbeam (Naval Academy graduate and former astronaut), and Glenard Middleton (president of American Federation of State, Country, and Municipal Employees [AFSCME] Local 44). These individuals and others have given the community reason to be proud that they are products of Turner Station.

The 1960s ushered in a challenging era of transition for the community in education as well as economics. Although the *Brown v. Board of Education* decision was rendered in 1954, its impact was not felt fully by Turner Station until the 1960s. Bragg (1964), Turner (1965), Sollers Point (1966), and Fleming schools (1968) were all closed, and students were transferred to integrated schools. The downside to this change was the loss of the close relationship between students and parents with teachers and administrators and the nurturing environment so characteristic of community schools. However, that decision also had an obvious long-term positive aspect as well, since African American students from Turner Station would have access to the same books, equipment, programs, and facilities available to the majority population.

With the demise of the American steel industry in the 1960s and the decline in U.S. manufacturing employment, the community experienced a steady erosion of jobs. The population declined from around 10,000 in the late 1950s to less than 3,000 today. Despite the change in fortunes and the challenges facing the community, there is an aggressive, ongoing effort to revitalize, grow, and return the community to its heritage of promise and achievement.

One

INDUSTRY

The old Maryland Steel Company's Sparrows Point plant is pictured in this 1890s photograph. The enormous rail yard complex can be seen, while the shipyard boardinghouse is visible in the distant left. The rail mill is on the right. (Courtesy of the BCPL Legacy Web.)

Bethlehem Steel Company's main office for the Sparrows Point plant is pictured in this October 1960 photograph. At its peak in the 1950s, the company employed approximately 30,000 workers at this location. (Courtesy of the BCPL Legacy Web.)

Bethlehem Steel's operations at Sparrows Point (above) date back to 1916. The facility was a major producer of steel and ships for the American war effort in World War II. During its heyday, the facility was the single largest employer of residents in Turner Station. The shipyard was sold in 1997, and the steel plant was sold in 2003. (Courtesy of the BCPL Legacy Web.)

The plate mill of the Bethlehem Steel Company is shown above during the 1950s. The Sparrows Point operation was a major employer in the Baltimore area. This was especially true for African American workers in the Turner Station community. (Courtesy of the BCPL Legacy Web.)

It is shift change at the steel plant. Workers are seen in 1956 leaving one of the many mills. The plant was a major employer, especially in the 1950s, when it accounted for over 30,000 well-paying jobs in the Baltimore area. (Courtesy of the BCPL Legacy Web.)

In this June 1956 photograph, Bethlehem Steel Company workers are seen walking the picket lines. Workers followed their unions in supporting this strike, which lasted for months. (Courtesy of the *Baltimore News-American*.)

Secretary of Labor Willard Wirtz meets with a group of protestors, including several members from the Turner Station community in 1967. These individuals had picketed the labor department building, protesting job discrimination at the Bethlehem Steel plant at Sparrows Point. The Reverend Shelton A. Fleming, a supervisor at the plant and pastor of Mount Olive Baptist Church, is standing on the far right. (Courtesy of the *Baltimore News-American*.)

A northbound No. 26 streetcar moves toward Turner Station after crossing the Bear Creek trestle. Bear Creek, Sparrows Point, and the opened trestle can be seen in the background of this 1950s photograph. (Courtesy of the Baltimore Streetcar Museum.)

Future GMC Safari and Chevy Astro minivans run the robotic gauntlet at the General Motors Corporation Broening Highway Plant in this 1988 photograph. The vehicles, which were once the mainstay of the company's small-van fleet, were later phased out of production. The plant closed in 2005, ending what was a major source of employment for the area. (Courtesy of the BCPL Legacy Web.)

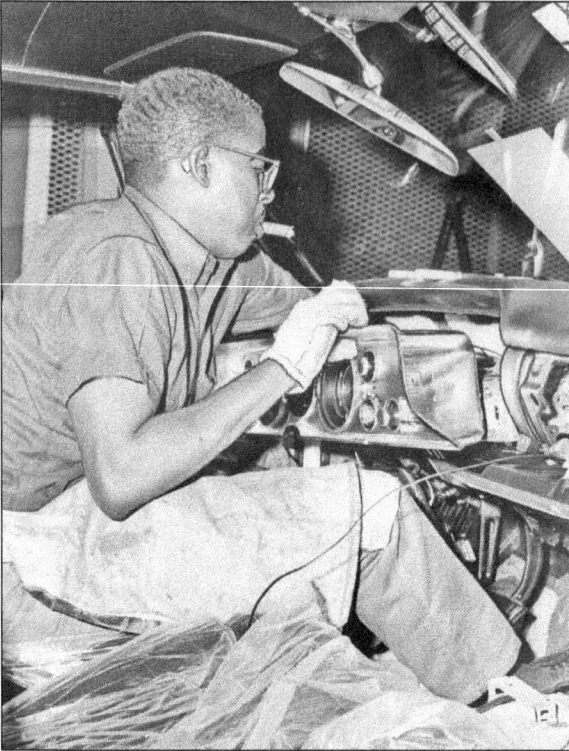

Willie Carter carefully inserts the instrument panel in the vehicle he is assembling in this 1964 photograph. Carter worked on the assembly line at the General Motors plant on Broening Highway. (Courtesy of the *Baltimore News-American*.)

Workers are busy assembling automobiles from the Chevrolet division in this 1960s photograph. They are part of the assembly line of the General Motors plant on Broening Highway. The company was a major employer in the Dundalk area, providing jobs to many from the Turner Station community. (Courtesy of the *Baltimore News-American*.)

The Baltimore Works of the Western Electric Company, above, was another of the major employers contributing to the job opportunities in the Turner Station community. (Courtesy of the *Baltimore News-American*.)

Workers are seen leaving the Western Electric plant following their shift in this 1960s photograph. (Courtesy of the *Baltimore News-American*.)

This 1940s shot shows the parking lot and facility of the Continental Can Company. Residents of Turner Station benefited from the presence of large manufacturers such as this within a short distance of the community. (Courtesy of the Afro-American Newspapers.)

This No. 26 streetcar is destined for Sparrows Point as it heads south near Turner Station. The streetcar passes the Riverside Power Plant on the left in this 1950s photograph. (Courtesy of the Baltimore Streetcar Museum.)

An employee appears atop one of Baltimore Gas and Electric Company's towers at Sollers Point in this 1977 shot. Bear Creek and Sparrows Point can be observed in the distance to the south. (Courtesy of the *Baltimore News-American*.)

This No. 26 streetcar has just crossed the Bear Creek Bridge, which connected Sparrows Point and Sollers Point. The electric substation to the right served to reduce voltage from the Riverside Power Plant to the 600 volts needed to power the streetcars. The No. 26 streetcar transported thousands of workers daily to and from Bethlehem Steel at Sparrows Point. (Courtesy of the Baltimore Streetcar Museum.)

The three-car train above is crossing Bear Creek between Sollers Point and Sparrows Point around 1937. The Bear Creek trestle provided much-needed direct rail access to the Bethlehem Steel plant from Baltimore. The span opened to allow pleasure craft to pass through. Both streetcars and railroad traffic utilized the span but on separate tracks. (Courtesy of Charles H. Echols Jr.)

Two

HOMES AND FAMILIES

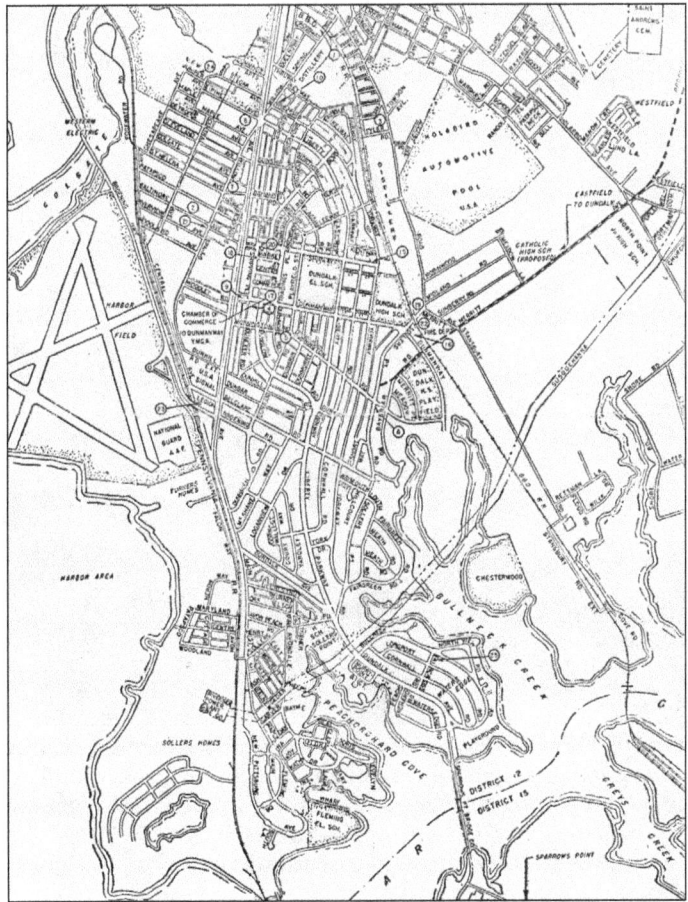

A 1950s map of the greater Dundalk area provides a view of the Turner Station community. Turner Homes was just below or south of the old Harbor Field (now the Dundalk Marine Terminal). Farther south and below the Riverside Power Plant was the Sollers Homes development. The current community is east of the railroad tracks and south of where Dundalk Avenue and Main Street intersect. It is bounded on the east by Peach Orchard Cove and on the south by Bear Creek. (Courtesy of the Afro-American Newspapers.)

A No. 26 streetcar traveling north from Sparrows Point passes by the stop near the Riverside Power Plant in this 1950s photograph. The Ernest Lyon development is on the left. (Courtesy of Herbert Harwood.)

Glenna Newton stands outside of the Turner Homes apartments holding Shirley James in this 1952 photograph. A baseball diamond is in the background on the left. Turner Homes was one of several housing developments in the Turner Station community. The homes were constructed by the federal government in 1942 in response to a critical shortage of housing for steelworkers at the Bethlehem Steel plant at Sparrows Point. The 199 apartment units were razed in the mid-1950s. (Courtesy of Lena James.)

Christine Roulhac stands outside the entrance to her apartment in the Turner Homes development in 1949. The war effort led to the construction of this and other similar developments in Turner Station in the 1940s due to the housing shortage. (Courtesy of Elsie Winston.)

The smiling youngsters in this 1930s pose are members of a group that attended Sunday school classes at the community center building at Turner Homes. The building was a multipurpose center used for a variety of activities by residents. (Courtesy of the BCPL Legacy Web.)

Sollers Homes was built in the 1940s to address the housing shortage created by the influx of workers at the steel mill and shipyard at Sparrows Point. The sign above describes the available housing and directs prospective renters to the rental office at 101 Breckenridge Drive in Turner Station. (Courtesy of the Afro-American Newspapers.)

A well-kept residence at 200 Stevenson Court is captured in this 1958 photograph. It is the home of the Harrison family. Charles Harrison, the head of household, was an employee of Bethlehem Steel at Sparrows Point. The family had resided in Sollers Homes since 1954. (Courtesy of the Afro-American Newspapers.)

Young men congregate at an unnamed corner in Sollers Homes in this 1950s photograph. The development was located just south of the Riverside Power Plant and west of the streetcar and railroad tracks. Individual housing units were one-, two-, or three-bedroom homes that rented for only $12 to $16 per week. (Courtesy of the Afro-American Newspapers.)

The construction site for the Ernest Lyon homes is pictured above. The development opened in 1942 under the local housing authority and consisted of 408 individual units with rental costs ranging from $48.50 to $58.50 per month. One-, two-, and three-bedroom homes were available to families in one- and two-story units. The development was named by the Federal Housing Authority in honor of Dr. Ernest Lyon (1860–1938), an African American minister, educator, journalist, and diplomat. (Courtesy of the BCPL Legacy Web.)

Young children of the Ernest Lyon development are shown above beautifying the area by planting trees in the community during the 1940s. The homes are visible in the background. (Courtesy of the BCPL Legacy Web.)

Members of the Mason family—Eleanor (left), Gloria (center), and Ronald—are at play near their home on New Pittsburg Avenue in the Ernest Lyon development. The homes can be seen in the background in this 1950s photograph. (Courtesy of Edie Brooks.)

This gentleman crosses the street at the intersection of Avondale Road, Sollers Point Road, and Avon Beach Road in the 1960s. This was one of the more heavily traveled areas of the community. (Courtesy of the *Baltimore News-American*.)

Alice Bobian tends her shrubbery at her residence on Avon Beach Road in this 1974 photograph. With her is her four-year old granddaughter, Cherise Roseman. She is also mother of the Bobian Four singing group. Her husband, Rev. King S. Bobian, an industrious man, built their one-story frame home in 1954 with the help of friends, family, and neighbors. (Courtesy of Shirley Bobian Macklin.)

Shepherd McDuffie Sr., a longtime resident of the community, cleans his car in front of his split-level home at 6 Henry Avenue in this 1972 photograph. He and his wife moved to Turner Station from South Carolina in 1945. He was employed by Bethlehem Steel until his retirement in 1983. (Courtesy of the *Baltimore News-American*.)

Standing in their yard at 124 Oak Street, Nannie Taylor and her children, Barbara (back left), Clarence, and Patricia, are preparing to attend morning worship services at church. They are dressed in their finest attire on this Easter Sunday in May 1956. (Courtesy of Patricia Taylor Brown.)

Clifton Jackson picks collards in his garden at his home at 130 Sollers Point Road in 1972. In 1951, he was the first African American to be appointed policeman in Baltimore County. Clifton was born in Sparrows Point, moved to Turner Station in the 1920s, and retired in 1971. (Courtesy of the *Baltimore News-American*.)

Homes along the 400 block of Chestnut Court are pictured in 1958. These homes were initially offered as public housing for war workers but were eventually sold to private families, many of whom were veterans. The corner home (left) belonged to Alexander Nixon and his wife, who migrated to Turner Station from North Carolina. (Courtesy of the Afro-American Newspapers.)

John and Rebecca Brice are seen in the living room of their Center Street home in Turner Station in 1952. Employed as a steel worker at Sparrows Point, John missed only one day of work in 45 years when he attended his father's funeral in South Carolina. (Courtesy of BCPL Legacy Web.)

The Day Village housing development shown above consisted of 500 two-bedroom units. It was opened in the late 1940s in response to the growing demand for housing due to the expanding work force at the Bethlehem Steel plant in nearby Sparrows Point. The development was named for the real estate developer Joseph P. Day. The housing units were built by the Ehrlich Development Corporation, which purchased the land from Joseph Day's widow. (Courtesy of the Afro-American Newspapers.)

Mack Jones Sr., his wife, and three children pose for this 1963 photograph outside their home in Day Village. Jones was one of the owners of the Jones Amoco Gas Station. (Courtesy of Mack Jones Sr.)

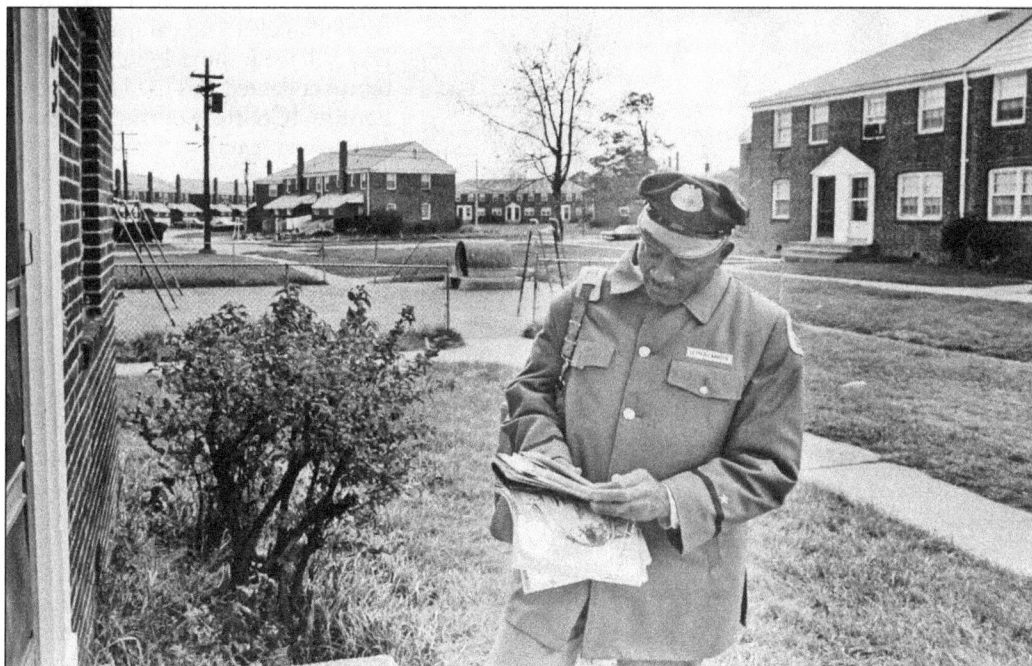

Vernon Wheadon was a postal worker in Turner Station for 13 years. On this clear day in May 1960, he is delivering mail on North Avondale Road in Day Village. (Courtesy of the *Baltimore News-American*.)

Members of Boy Scout Troop 270 conduct a clean-up campaign in Day Village in June 1963. The refuse collected was used for a huge bonfire. (Courtesy of the *Baltimore News-American*.)

Iris and Charles (Chappie) Manning are celebrating their 50th anniversary in this 2005 picture. Charles came to Turner Station during World War II from Hamlet, North Carolina, and Iris migrated to Turner Station from Roanoke, Virginia, in 1940. Chappie was a light heavyweight boxing champion and was inducted in the Boxing Hall of Fame in 1985. Iris and Chappie were both active in election campaigns. Iris served on the Democratic State Central Committee from 1987 to 1990. (Courtesy of Iris Manning.)

This picture of the attractive couple Frank and Jennie Jordan, was taken around 1915 in Philadelphia, Pennsylvania. John and Grace Jordan, with their mother Jennie Jordan, pose at right at the photographer's studio in 1919. The Jordans moved to Turner Station in 1926. The couple had six children. (Both courtesy of Rhonda Quarles.)

This picture of Frank and Jennie's daughter, Grace Jordan Quarles, with her oldest daughter, Margaret, was taken around 1936. (Courtesy of Rhonda Quarles.)

Frank and Jennie Jordan purchased a new shingle bungalow home at 122 Center Street for $3,300 on March 24, 1925, as this mortgage agreement indicates. (Courtesy of Rhonda Quarles.)

Frank and Jennie Jordan resided at 122 Center Street, where they raised their six children. Their granddaughter, Rhonda Quarles, renovated the home, built in 1925, and currently lives there. (Courtesy of Rhonda Quarles.)

Three

SCHOOLS AND EDUCATION

These Turner Station students are being assisted and directed by the crossing guard on Center Street in this December 1941 photograph. (Courtesy of the Afro-American Newspapers.)

Turner Elementary, the first public school in Turner Station, was originally a two-room portable building constructed in the summer of 1925. A permanent facility was built on a 2.5-acre tract on Oak Street in 1930. Only two principals—Addison Pinckney (1925–1945) and Frances Bruce (1945–1965)—served at the school during its 40-year existence. Turner Elementary closed on June 30, 1965. After serving briefly as a child development center in 1966 and 1967, it is now a senior citizens' apartment building. (Courtesy the BCPL Legacy Web.)

Turner Elementary School students are seen above participating in a festive springtime outdoor activity as parents and school staff look on. The young man in the foreground of this 1950s photograph, Skip Wade, is the son of a local physician, Dr. William C. Wade. Turner was one of two elementary schools in the community. (Courtesy of the BCPL Legacy Web.)

A group of former teachers and administrators from Turner Elementary School appear at this 1950s function. From left to right are former principal Frances Bruce, teacher Lois Gilmore Smith, retired teacher Francis Proctor, and first principal Addison Pinckney. (Courtesy of the BCPL Legacy Web.)

On May 6, 1958, this well-disciplined group of students stands on the steps of Turner Elementary School. This safety patrol was one of the best trained to be found anywhere. Students were selected in the first grade for certain errand duties and worked their way up. Moses Pounds, top row, far left, was patrol captain. (Courtesy of the Afro-American Newspapers.)

Fleming Elementary, the second school to be built in Turner Station, opened in 1944. Located in the Ernest Lyon housing development, it was constructed on a 2.5-acre parcel of land. It was named for Philip Bracken Fleming, the head of the Federal Works Agency, which was responsible for its funding and construction. The school provided primary education for the youth of Turner Station from 1944 until its closing in 1968. (Courtesy of the Afro-American Newspapers.)

Three teachers at the Turner Station Community Center appear in this 1957 photograph. They taught third- and fourth-grade classes here for Fleming Elementary School due to overcrowding at the school. They are, from left to right, Katherine Patterson, second-grade teacher; Dorothy McKinner, art instructor, who visited several county schools; and Josephine Flournoy, third-grade teacher. (Courtesy of the Afro-American Newspapers.)

36

An eager group of young elementary school children are captured in this 1955 photograph at Fleming Elementary School. Thelma Stanley-Sterrett is the teacher of this class of first-grade students. Stanley-Sterrett was also the author's first-grade teacher. (Courtesy of Shirley Bobian-Macklin.)

In May 1958, these young members of the newly formed Library Club of America, Inc., at Fleming Elementary School, learn to appreciate reading at an early age. The librarian, Hortense L. Hackett, was the advisor. Seen with the pupils is Arlyn Sweeney. (Courtesy of the Afro-American Newspapers.)

Busy youngsters are shown in the 1950s on the lawn in front of the Fleming Elementary School. The activities were part of the school's annual May Day Festival, as the king and queen can be seen in the background. (Courtesy of Maxine Waterhouse Thompson.)

This was the first public elementary school for African American students in Sparrows Point. The school opened around 1890 and was located at Sixth and J Streets. Flooding of Humphrey's Creek in 1927 resulted in extensive damage to the original building. An entirely new facility (below), constructed at Tenth and J Streets, was named in honor of the Reverend George Freeman Bragg, rector of St. James Episcopal Church in Baltimore City. Reverend Bragg was an African American author, educator, and journalist. The school served elementary, middle, and high school students at various times during its existence. Students from Turner Station, Sparrows Point, Edgemere, and Norris Lane were bussed to Bragg for grades five and six from 1948 to 1964. The school closed in 1964. The building was purchased by Bethlehem Steel in 1965 and used for offices until 1974, when it was demolished. (Courtesy of the BCPL Legacy Web.)

These teachers are gathered outside the entrance to the George F. Bragg School in Sparrows Point in the 1950s. With the opening of Sollers Point High School in Turner Station, Bragg returned to being an elementary school. Students were bussed from Turner Station, Chase, Edgemere, and other nearby communities for grades five and six before going on to high school in Turner Station. (Courtesy of the BCPL Legacy Web.)

Students and teachers from the George F. Bragg School observe Fire Prevention Week in October 1951. They received fire safety instruction, a tour of a fire station, and demonstrations on the use of fire department equipment. (Courtesy of the Dundalk–Patapsco Neck Historical Society.)

40

Under the close scrutiny of their instructor, Elizabeth Williams, students from the class of 1948 complete a written assignment in French. This group would be the last class to graduate from the George F. Bragg High School, as the new Sollers Point Junior-Senior High School would open in the fall of 1948 in nearby Turner Station. (Courtesy of Charles and Veronica Mandy.)

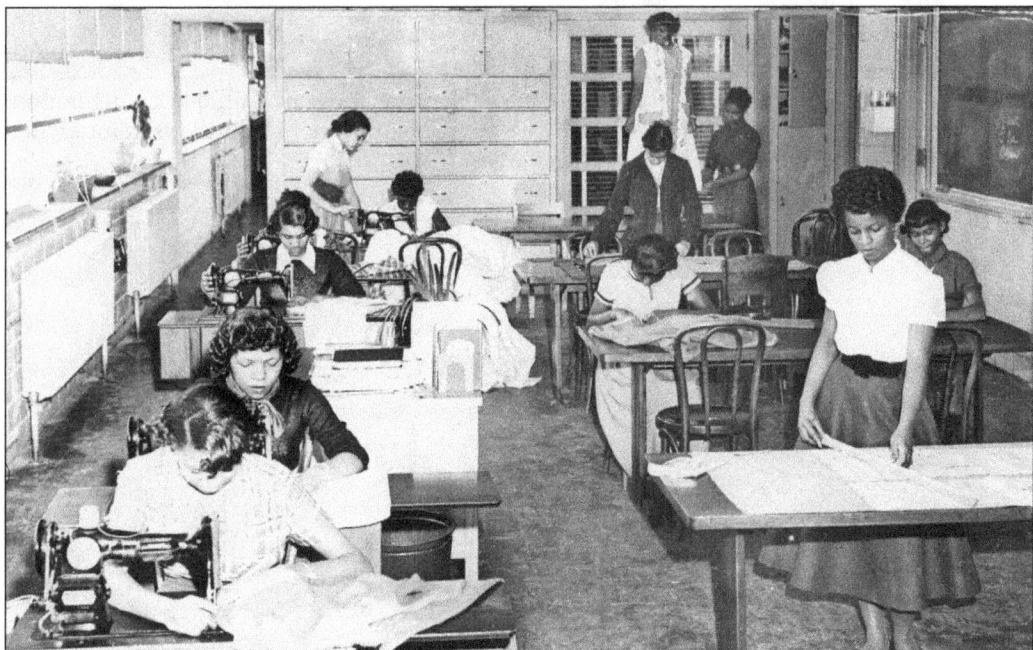

Members of the class of 1953 are pictured above applying their training in the art of sewing and making clothes. Home economics classes were an important part of the curriculum for young African American women at Sollers Point High School. (Courtesy of Charles and Veronica Mandy.)

These young ladies demonstrate their athletic skills as they pose in a unique configuration. They were members of a gymnastics class at the Bragg High School in Sparrows Point around 1948–1949. (Courtesy of Charles and Veronica Mandy.)

In this 1947 photograph, workmen drive piles in preparation for laying the foundation for the million-dollar Sollers Point High School. Having the school in the community meant local students would no longer have to travel 12 miles to Baltimore or cross Bear Creek to Sparrows Point for their secondary school training. The site was formerly occupied by the Edgewater Beach. (Courtesy of the Afro-American Newspapers.)

Sollers Point High School opened in 1948. Located at 325 Sollers Point Road, it was built on a 7-acre tract near the intersection of Dundalk Avenue and Sollers Point Road (formerly the site of the Edgewater Beach). While the student body was primarily from Turner Station, students were also bussed in from nearby communities. Enrollment was around 300 initially and peaked at nearly 900 by 1958. Today it is a technical high school. (Courtesy of the BCPL Legacy Web.)

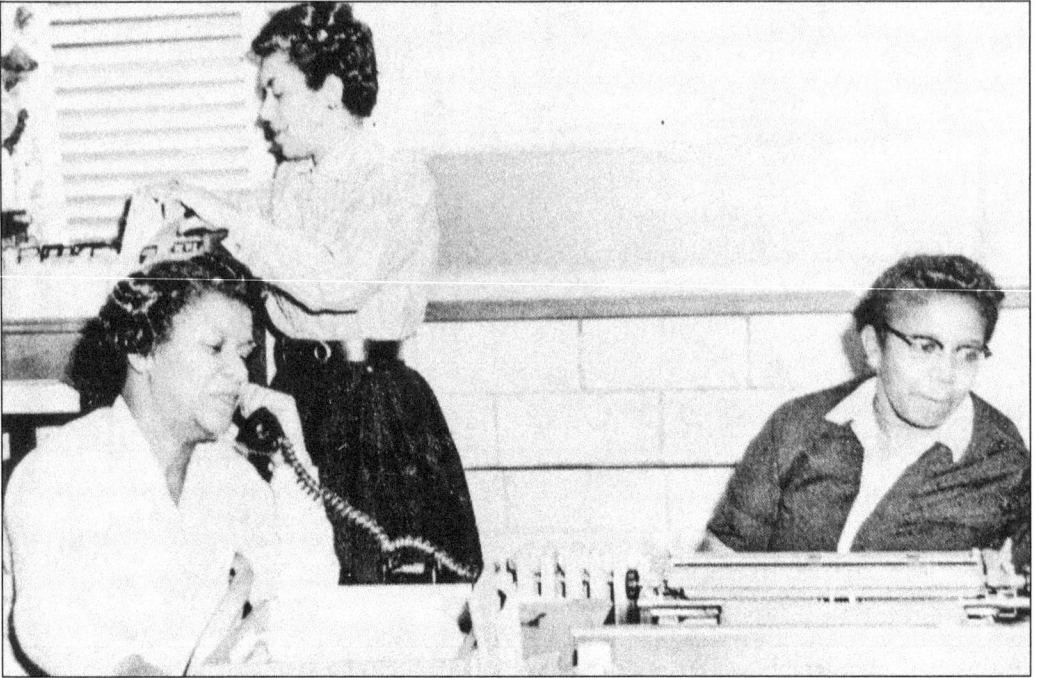

Members of the Sollers Point High School secretarial staff are busy filing, typing, and answering the telephone in this 1960 photograph. Responsible for maintaining an efficient office, the staff assisted the administration in transacting its business. Shown above from left to right are Naomi Jenkins, Florence Brown, and Elizabeth Randall. (Courtesy of the BCPL Legacy Web.)

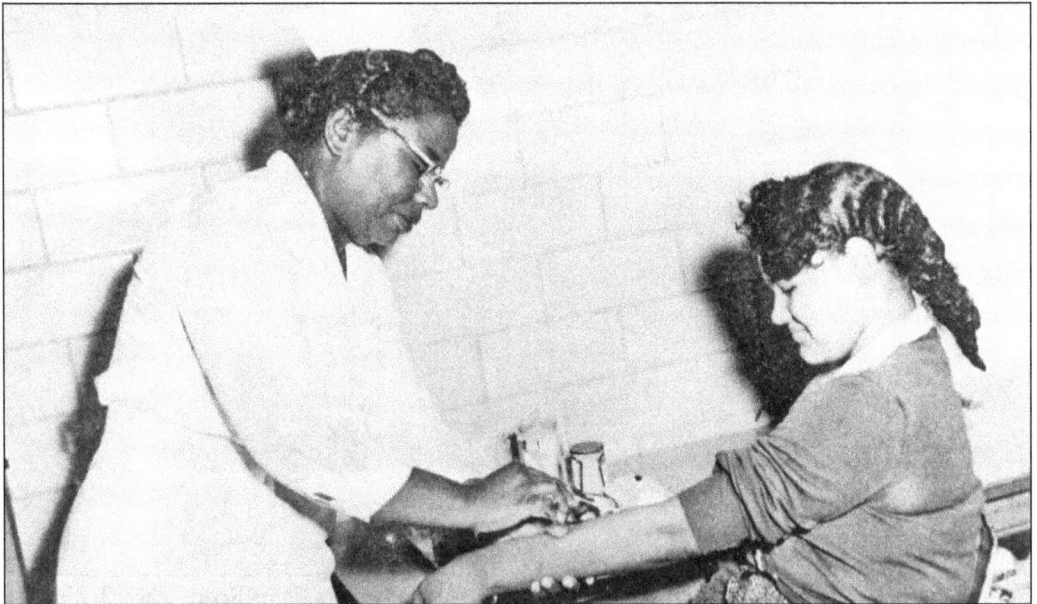

The school nurse was a key member of the Sollers Point High School staff. As head of the health department, she tended to students' medical needs while maintaining important medical records of the students she saw on a daily basis. Delores Lynch receives medical attention from Daisy Gwynn in this 1961 photograph. (Courtesy of the BCPL Legacy Web.)

Students could always look forward to the lunch hour at Sollers Point. Led by Della Lemon (manager), the cafeteria staff in 1961 included Ida Drewitt (left) and Viola Harris (right). (Courtesy of the BCPL Legacy Web.)

Keeping the school clean was the mission of the custodial staff at Sollers, headed by Rudolph Hurt, the chief custodian. Hurt and Ada Vaughn appear in the school cafeteria in this 1960 photograph. The full staff consisted of six individuals. (Courtesy of the BCPL Legacy Web.)

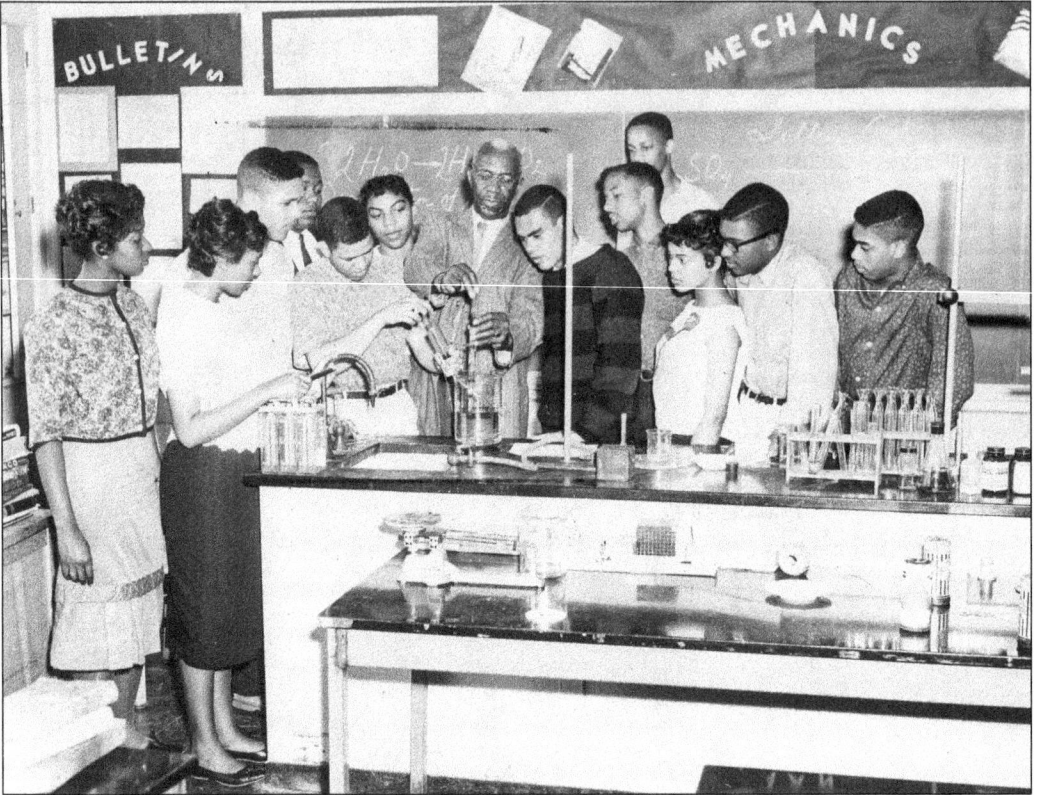

Members of the 12A class of 1960 closely observe as their instructor, Richard Ryan, conducts a physics experiment. Classroom experiments were a practical application of the formulas and theorems discussed in class. (Courtesy of the Afro-American Newspapers.)

Young ladies practice homemaking skills in their home economics class at Sollers Point High School. They utilize electric stoves and other modern equipment in this 1960 lab phase of the program. (Courtesy of the BCPL Legacy Web.)

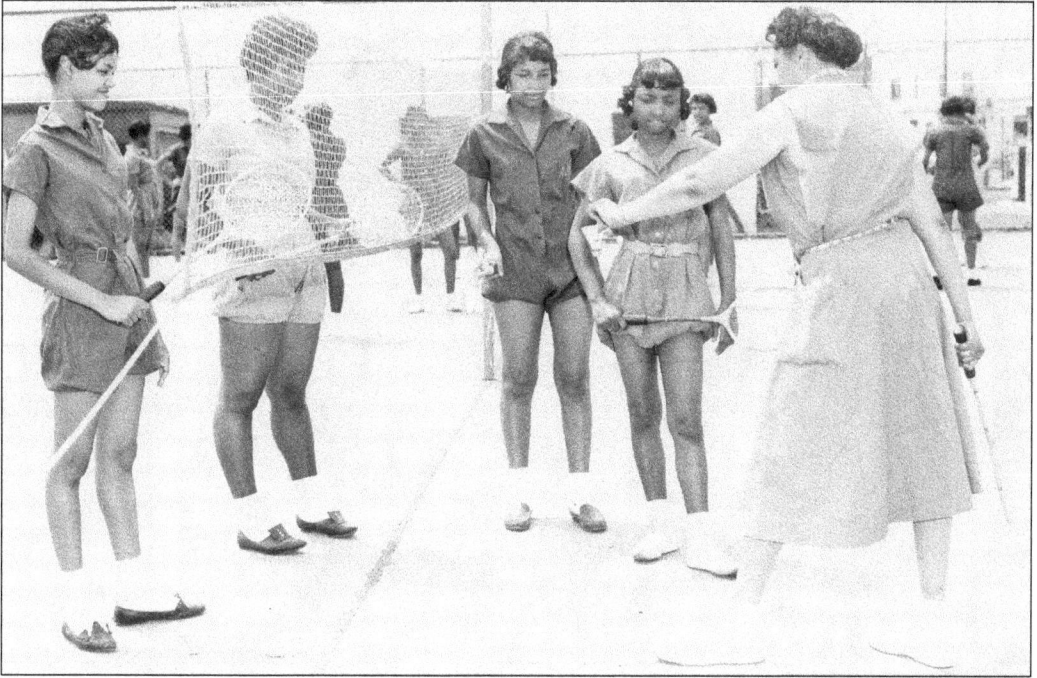

In this 1960 photograph, Annie Gittings (right), a physical education instructor at Sollers Point High School, gives pointers to these 10th-grade students on how to play badminton. From left to right, the pupils are Cecilia Watkins, Victoria Curbeam, Andrea McCormick, and Cleo Orr. (Courtesy of the Afro-American Newspapers.)

Young women from the Sollers Point High School 12AC class display their form before their instructor Annie Gittings (left). Archery classes such as this were divided into small groups. These students are receiving instructions in the fundamental steps for a right-handed archer. Class participants are, from left to right, Delphina Thomas, Rosetta Scott, Arnedia Brown, and unidentified, all seniors from the class of 1960. (Courtesy of Charles and Veronica Mandy.)

Sports were an integral part of the extra-curricular activities at Sollers. The 1960 Varsity Basketball Team, the "Trojans," is pictured above. Members of the squad are (standing) G. McGuire (manager), L. Lewis, R. Evans, R. McCormick, O. Robertson, G. Washington, and L. Faidley (manager); (kneeling) J. Curbeam, E. Godsey, M. Evans, and R. Jones. (Courtesy of the BCPL Legacy Web.)

The Sollers Point High School varsity track and field team members are shown in a 1962 group photograph clad in their warm-up outfits. The school maintained an enviable reputation and status among Baltimore County and Maryland state high school track teams, winning numerous titles and awards over the years. (Courtesy of Charles and Veronica Mandy.)

One of the greatest moments in sports for Sollers Point High School came in 1950. The elite foursome of, left to right, Louis Winston, Alvin Bagley, Harry Pugh, and Frank Randolph was awarded the Gold Medal for winning the prestigious mile relay during the Penn Relays in Philadelphia, Pennsylvania. The team repeated as winners in this event in 1951 and 1952. (Courtesy of the BCPL Legacy Web.)

J. Bruce Turner, athletics director at Sollers Point High School, identifies some of the outstanding track and basketball players he has coached over the years. Charles Fletcher, the school principal (right), is also seen in this May 1958 shot. The school had one of the best track and field programs in the state of Maryland. (Courtesy of the Afro-American Newspapers.)

Varsity track team members from Sollers Point High School are seen above with Baltimore County executive Spiro T. Agnew in 1964. The team was recognized for being Baltimore County mile relay champions during the 1964 track season. Team members are, from left to right, McArthur McGowens, Ernest Evans, Jerry Alston, Earl Wake, and Alvin McArthur. The track coach is Reginald Holt (second from the right). (Courtesy of Carolyn McArthur.)

Members of this dance group perform in the musical *Sweet Anne Page* at Sollers Point High School in 1953. Musicals and short plays were notable aspects of the school's extracurricular activities. (Courtesy of Charles and Veronica Mandy.)

High-stepping members of the 1960 Sollers Point High School majorettes were a part of the schools award-winning band. The majorettes are, from left to right, B. House, G. Jones, M. Hayes, G. McMorris, V. Waddell, S. Scott (drum majorette), S. Lynch, V. Faidley, M. Lassiter, H. Taylor, J. Owens, and G. Gaines. (Courtesy of the BCPL Legacy Web.)

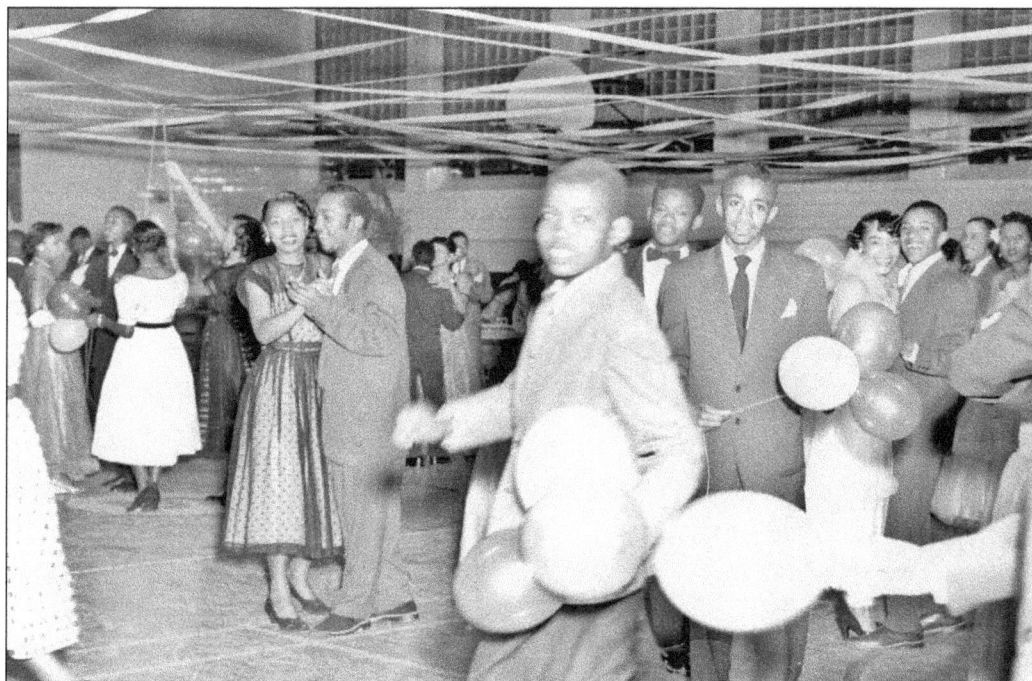

It is an evening of gaiety and fun as young couples dance the night away. Members of the class of 1952 celebrate and enjoy the great music and memorable moments of their annual school prom. (Courtesy of Charles and Veronica Mandy.)

These young men, dressed in their formal attire, strike a classy pose at the high school prom in the spring of 1962. They are, from left to right, Robert Pearl, David Rice, Reginald Flournoy, Archie Blackwell, and Charles Fleming, all graduating seniors. (Courtesy of the BCPL Legacy Web.)

Senior Beulah Newton, escorted by fellow classmate John Powell, reigns as Miss Sollers Point in this 1960 photograph. Each year, Miss Sollers Point represented the school at the annual Homecoming football game at Morgan State College. (Courtesy of Beulah Newton-Williamson.)

Members of the 1949 graduating class from Sollers Point High School are shown with their principal, Charles W. Fletcher. The 43 eleventh graders were the first to matriculate from the newly opened school and also the only class to do so under the old graduation requirements. Beginning with the 1949–1950 academic year, students were required to complete 12 years of education in order to graduate from high school in Baltimore County. (Courtesy of the BCPL Legacy Web.)

Principal Charles W. Fletcher (seated in center) is shown above with proud members of the graduating class of 1952. This group was only the third class to matriculate under the new graduation rules requiring 12 years of formal education in Baltimore County. (Courtesy of Charles and Veronica Mandy.)

Four

CHURCH AND WORSHIP

A No. 26 streetcar approaches the crossing at Maryland Avenue in Turner Station. The streetcar was a principal means of transportation to and from the Bethlehem Steel Company mill and shipyard operations at Sparrows Point. Residents depended on the streetcar to travel not only to "the point," but also to Dundalk and destinations in Baltimore City. Main Street parallels the streetcar tracks on the left. St. Matthews Methodist Church, one of several churches in the community, is also on the left in the foreground. Churches played a prominent role in the spiritual and cultural growth of Turner Station. (Courtesy of Herbert Harwood.)

The first church in the community was organized and founded in 1900 by a group of Christian workers led by a local street preacher, John Moore. St. Matthews was organized in the home of Marie Harris. The cornerstone of the original church, located in the Meadow (the corner of Dundalk Avenue and Main Street), was laid on May 1, 1910. The present-day church was built on Avon Beach Road and Main Street in 1937. (Courtesy of the BCPL Legacy Web.)

Reverend and Mrs. Leslie Dyson (center) are with the St. Matthews United Methodist Church Council of Ministries in this 1977 photograph. The council consisted of the leaders of key church auxiliaries. (Courtesy of Oliver Riddick.)

A young group of singers known as the Harmonette Choir is shown in this 1950s photograph. They are members of the congregation at St. Matthews United Methodist Church. Their leaders are Emma Franklin (rear left) and Barbara Newton (rear right). The pastor, Reverend John H. Carter, stands on the right in this 1950s photograph. (Courtesy of Shirley Bobian Macklin.)

The New Shiloh Baptist Church, located at 105 East Avenue, was founded in July 1931. The Reverend David Bryant was the founder and first pastor. The church was the second congregation to come into existence in the community. The building seen here was the church's first edifice and was built in 1934. It was replaced in 1971. Today New Shiloh Baptist Church has one of the community's largest congregations. (Courtesy of Charles and Veronica Mandy.)

The Reverend James Everett stands outside the New Shiloh Baptist Church at 105 East Avenue in this 1970s shot. Reverend Everett was installed as pastor in 1953 and served until his passing in 1988. He presided over the construction of a new edifice in 1971. (Courtesy of the *Baltimore News-American*.)

The Young Adult Choir of New Shiloh Baptist Church appears in this 1953 photograph. The group inspired the congregation on Sunday mornings with their melodious renditions of hymns. (Courtesy of Oliver Riddick.)

Senior Usher Board members appear on the steps at the entrance to New Shiloh Baptist Church in Turner Station in this 1950s photograph. Ocie Knuckles was president of the female ushers, and Ernest Collona led the male ushers. (Courtesy of Oliver Riddick.)

The First Apostolic Faith Gospel Tabernacle Church was founded in 1931 by the late Bishop George Levant. The congregation worshipped in the home of one of its members and at other makeshift locations for several years. Finally, in 1935, a permanent church building was erected at the corner of Balnew and Ash Streets where the church resides today. (Courtesy of Charles H. Echols Jr.)

The original edifice of the Gospel Tabernacle Church is seen in this 1994 photograph. The new wing of the church extends out to the right and was constructed in 1988. (Courtesy of Charles H. Echols Jr.)

Members of the Gospel Tabernacle Church gather on the lawn of the church in this August 1954 photograph. The occasion was the ninth convocation (revival) of the church. (Courtesy of the First Apostolic Faith Gospel Tabernacle Church.)

Friendship Baptist Church was founded by the late Rev. Dockery S. Thompson. The church was first located at 411 New Pittsburgh Avenue in the Ernest Lyon development. Reverend Thompson served as pastor for 45 years (1948–1993). The congregation currently worships at 307.5 Avondale Road. (Courtesy of Charles H. Echols Jr.)

This 1960s photograph shows the original home of the Friendship Baptist Church. The congregation worshipped here from 1954 until the new building was constructed in 1962. (Courtesy of the Friendship Baptist Church.)

Members of the Friendship Baptist Church are in service with their pastor, Rev. Dockery S. Thompson, in this 1960s photograph. (Courtesy of Grace Bryant.)

Located at 209 Walnut Street, the Greater St. John Baptist Church was founded in 1952. It came into being as a result of a split with its mother church, the New Shiloh Baptist Church. The Reverend David Benjamin Banks led the new congregation after having served as pastor of New Shiloh since 1940. (Courtesy of Charles H. Echols Jr.)

Rev. David Banks leads the congregation of the Greater St. John Baptist Church in this ground-breaking service in 1953. This launched the construction of the congregation's first church building. (Courtesy of the Greater St. John Baptist Church.)

This is the first church one encounters (on the right) traveling north after the Francis Scott Key Bridge. Founded in 1955, Mount Olive was initially housed in the old community building until a new edifice was erected in 1980. The church has had only two pastors during its 53-year history: the founder Rev. Shelton A. Fleming and Rev. Carlton S. Lewis. (Courtesy of Charles H. Echols Jr.)

Mount Olive Baptist Church, seen in this 1962 photograph, was housed in the old community building. The building served as a recreation center and as an extension to Fleming Elementary School during the 1950s. (Courtesy of the Mount Olive Baptist Church.)

64

Rev. Shelton A. Fleming, pastor of the Mount Olive Baptist Church, is shown in the pulpit during a service in 1980. Fleming, who was supervisor at the shipyard in Sparrows Point, served the congregation from 1955 until 1990. (Courtesy of the Mount Olive Baptist Church.)

Church members and friends from Mount Olive Baptist Church pose in this 1960s photograph. The group enjoyed an outing to the Luray Caverns near Front Royal, Virginia. Kneeling on the right is the church's founder and pastor, Rev. Shelton. A. Fleming. (Courtesy of Dunbar Brooks.)

A mission of St. Francis Xavier Church, Christ the King Catholic Church was founded by the Josephite Fathers to serve the Turner Station community in 1956. It also served the Watersedge and Logan Village communities. Due to declining membership, the church closed just after the beginning of the 21st century. (Courtesy of Charles H. Echols Jr.)

A view of the altar of Christ the King Catholic Church is captured in this 1957 photograph. The occasion was the dedication of the church by the archbishop of Baltimore, Francis P. Keough. (Courtesy of the BCPL Legacy Web.)

The oldest congregation in Turner Station is that of Union Baptist Church. In existence since 1893, it was founded in Sparrows Point. After the expansion of the Bethlehem Steel plant in 1972, the church relocated to Turner Station. Today it occupies the old Anthony Theater building at 105 Main Street. (Courtesy of Charles H. Echols Jr.)

The building above was the original location of Union Baptist Church on Ninth and J Streets in Sparrows Point. The congregation worshipped here from March 1913 until they moved to Turner Station in 1972. (Courtesy of Union Baptist Church.)

Tas and Bettie Cragway Statham were faithful members of the Union Baptist Church. They raised an outstanding family in Sparrows Point. Tas was probably the first black officially hired as a foreman at Bethlehem Steel in Sparrows Point. The *Baltimore News-American* recognized the couple for educating each of their six children. Walter, Calvin, Clara, and Betty Statham were all college-trained musicians. Robert and Mack graduated from Morgan State College and Hampton Institute respectively. (Courtesy of Calvin and Malvilyn Statham.)

Ladies from the Order of the Eastern Star are shown above in 1960. The unidentified gentleman is a Mason. (Courtesy of the BCPL Legacy Web.)

Five

BUSINESS

A cluster of small businesses can be viewed on Main Street in this 1950s photograph. The Anthony Theater, a general cleaners, and a television repair shop can be seen as one looks north along the street. Numerous small businesses owned by Turner Station residents were located throughout the community. (Courtesy of the Afro-American Newspapers.)

The Anthony Theater, which opened in late 1946, was located at 103 South Main Street. The modern 700-seat, air-conditioned, state-of-the-art facility was financed and built by Dr. Joseph Thomas and named in honor of his father, Anthony. The theater was managed by Flavia Thomas and remained open until attendance declined in the mid-1950s with the advent of television. (Courtesy of the BCPL Legacy Web.)

This stucco building, located at the intersection of Main Street and Sollers Point Road, was home to a variety of businesses. The building in this 1947 photograph included a barbershop, drugstore, and cleaning company on the first floor and two apartments on the second floor. To the right of the building is the Anthony Theater. (Courtesy of the Afro-American Newspapers.)

Zelma Strawther of 135 Carver Road does the family wash at the newly opened General Cleaners Laundromat at 107 Sollers Point Road in Turner Station on May 14, 1960. (Courtesy of the Afro-American Newspapers.)

The Acme Market served residents of Day Village as well as patrons along Avondale Road. Customers are being waited on by Terry Florence, a store clerk, in this 1947 shot. (Courtesy of the *Baltimore News-American*.)

This 1960s photograph looks north from the entrance to Day Village. The Village Drugstore is on the right. Farther along that same side of the street were the Acme Market, the rental and maintenance office, and a gas station and candy store. (Courtesy of the Afro-American Newspapers.)

Gloria Mason is shown sitting behind the counter in her position as clerk at the Village Drugstore as a customer approaches on the right in this 1950s photograph. The drugstore was not only a favorite hangout for youth but was also often a source of employment. (Courtesy of Dunbar Brooks.)

Phyllis Strawther and a friend are having lunch at the Day Village Drugstore in this 1953 photograph. The drugstore, one of several in the community, provided prescription drugs, ice cream, candy, and many other products and services. (Courtesy of Maxine Waterhouse Thompson.)

Haywood Bryant had operated this service station on Avondale Road for 14 months at the time of this photograph. He was typical of the young businessmen who offer goods and services to residents of the thriving community in the early 1960s. (Courtesy of the Afro-American Newspapers.)

The Ford taxicab shown above during the 1940s was owned by the Balnew Cab Company. It was one of several local companies providing taxi services to the Turner Station community. (Courtesy of the BCPL Legacy Web.)

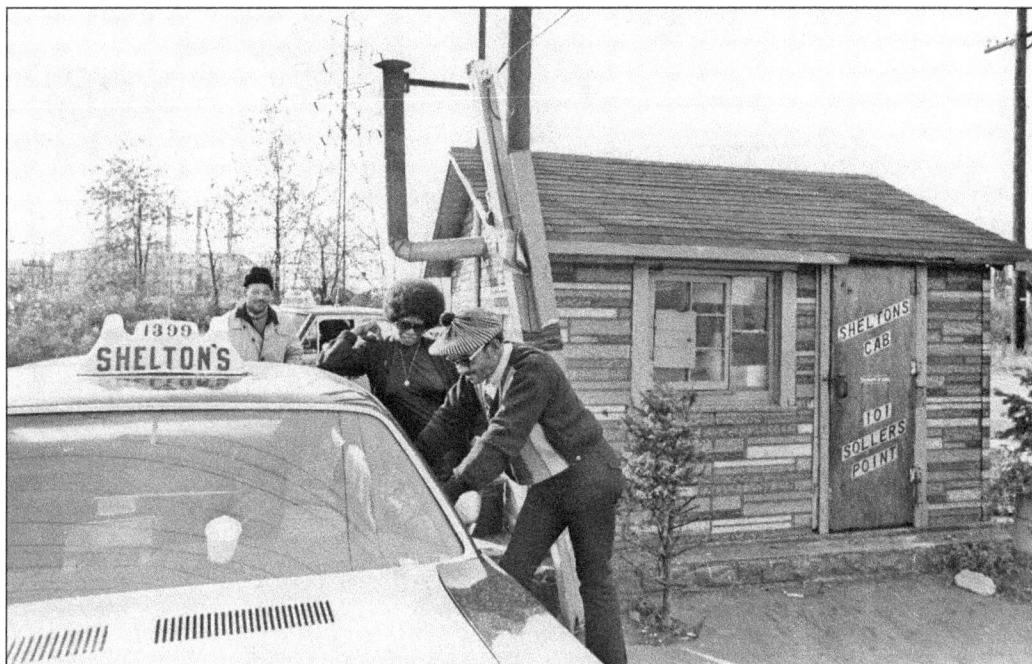

Shelton's Cab Company was one of many locally owned and operated small businesses found in Turner Station. James Shelton, the owner, is seen here at the cabstand at 101 Sollers Point Road. Several of his cabs are visible. Shelton moved to Turner Station in 1939 from South Carolina and worked for several years at Bethlehem Steel before opening Shelton's Cab Company, the first of several businesses, in 1941. He also owned an Amoco Station, a coal business, and a charter bus company. Shelton's Cab Company later became the Atwater Cab Company and served the community for over 40 years. A business card promoting the services of Shelton's Cab Company appears below. (Courtesy of the Afro-American Newspaper.)

Vivian Carrington of 751 South Avondale Road drove 500 miles a week as a cab driver in Turner Station in the early 1960s. She worked with Shelton Cabs for 10 years. Her husband, John Carrington, worked at Sparrows Point. Their children are LaVerne, 13, a pupil at Sollers Point High School, and Cynthia, 12, who attended Bragg Elementary School. (Courtesy of the Afro-American Newspapers.)

This ambitious young businessman, Luke Durant, resided at 126 Chestnut Street. Luke worked for the Afro-American Newspapers as an Afro carrier. He takes a break from his grass-cutting chores to read about Roy Rogers in this 1960s photograph. (Courtesy of the Afro-American Newspapers.)

Peter Douglass of 115 Willow Court, Day Village, enjoys listening to an LP record in this 1960s photograph. Members of the Douglass family had sold the Afro-American Newspapers in the community as early as 1946. (Courtesy of the Afro-American Newspapers.)

Thomas Allmond, proprietor of Allmond's Grocery Store, is seen with a customer, Elsie Winston, in this 1950s photograph. The business was located at 201 Main Street across from the St. Matthews Methodist Church and provided a much-needed service for decades. (Courtesy of the *Baltimore News-American*.)

Rosetta Hill handles a customer's purchase in this 1960 photograph. Hill's Grocery Store was one of the larger businesses in the community. The store was located at 118 Oak Avenue in a cluster of businesses that included a barbershop, a pool hall, a five-and-dime store, and a package goods store. The grocery store was a vital enterprise for the community and had been operated by Anthony and Rosetta Hill since 1948. (Courtesy of the Afro-American Newspapers.)

The Balnew building, located on Oak Avenue and Main Street, was built and owned by the Balnew Improvement Association, a group of pioneering residents led by Edward Hill in the 1930s. They promoted black businesses, improved community lighting, completed the sewage, and installed street signs and house numbering. On the second floor was a pool hall and teen center. Downstairs were Hill's Grocery Store, the Ranch, Dorsey's Photography, a hat store, and Jimmy's Barber Shop. (Courtesy of the Afro-American Newspapers.)

Mary Brice McCormick sits on the steps in front of the Wyatt Grocery Store in the 1940s. Located at Sollers Point Road and Pine Street, the store was one of many small local businesses that operated in the community. (Courtesy of the BCPL Legacy Web.)

The truck above was used by Mondie's Cleaners to pick up and deliver clothes to customers. George and Alice Mondie (below) moved to Turner Station in 1946. Their business, which opened in 1953, was located at Avondale Road for a while and later located at Avon Beach Road. Mondie retired in 1984 after being in business for nearly 30 years. (Courtesy of the Mondie family.)

James A. Morton II, a former resident of Turner Station, became a mortician in the late 1940s. In 1954, he and Leroy O. Dyett opened the Morton and Dyett Funeral Homes. In the 1960s, he constructed a funeral home at Main Street in Turner Station. He is the founder and chief executive officer of James A. Morton and Sons Funeral Homes, Inc., and has served as president of the Funeral Directors and Morticians Association of Maryland. (Courtesy of James A. Morton II.)

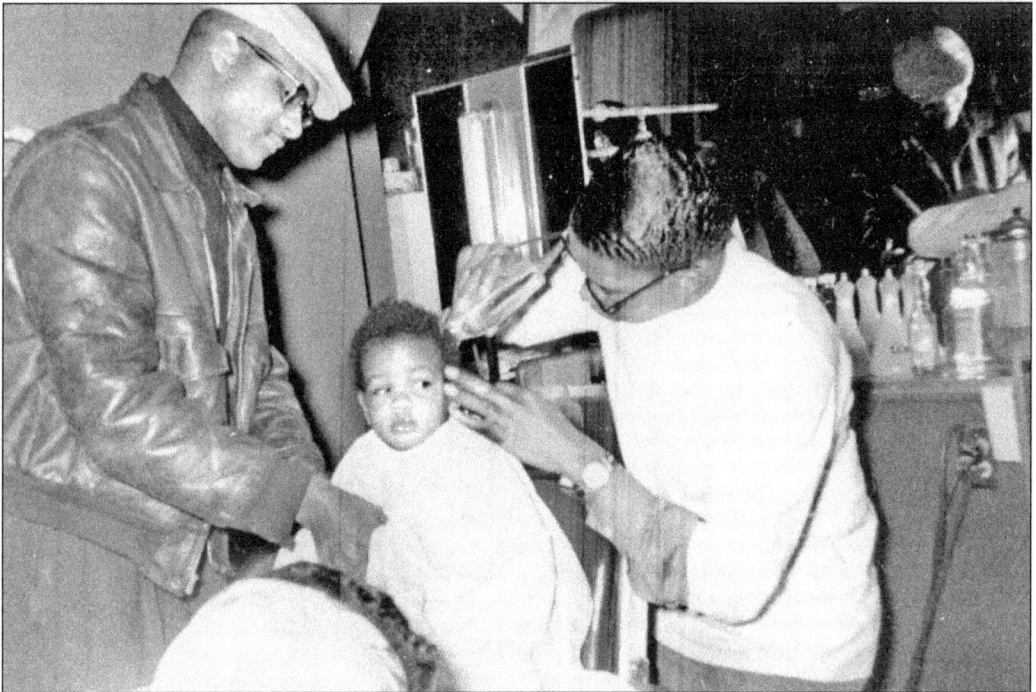

Young Steven Wynn gets his very first haircut from Mr. Mitchell at Speed's Barber Shop in Turner Station. His father, Samuel Wynn, looks on. The shop, owned by John Speed, was located at 201 (Second Rear) Main Street. (Courtesy of Courtney Speed.)

The late John Emmett Speed Jr. is pictured above in the Day Village area in 1958. Speed, a community leader and businessman, was owner of Speed's Barber Shop on Main Street. His business still thrives under the capable hands of Zellious Allen, Margaret Watkins, and the Speed family. (Courtesy of Priscilla Williams.)

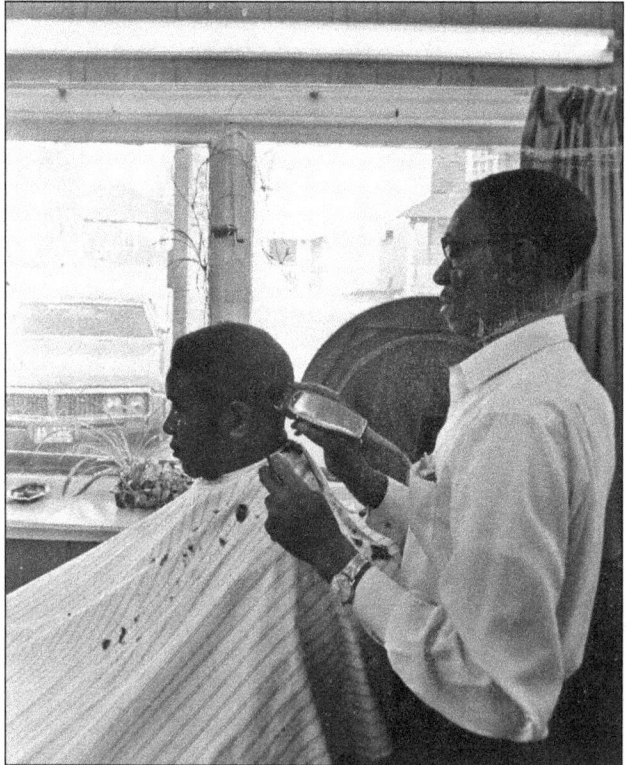

Ollie Harris trims a customer's hair in this 1950s shot. His shop was located on Avondale Road across from the track and grounds of Sollers Point High School. This was one of several barbershops in the community. (Courtesy of the Afro-American Newspapers.)

Irvin Adams, owner of Adams Cocktail Lounge, is seen above in his establishment. Izrea Simon is on the right. Adams came to Turner Station in 1909. Following the repeal of Prohibition, he opened a liquor store in 1933, expanded it to a bar in 1938, and added a dining room, lounge, and stage in the 1940s. The establishment became one of the most popular black clubs in Baltimore County, drawing big bands and attractions from the East Coast circuit. (Courtesy of the BCPL Legacy Web.)

This rundown-looking building that was once Adams Bar and Cocktail Lounge on Balnew Avenue is pictured in 1994. The once-famous establishment closed in the 1980s. It was foreclosed by Baltimore County due to unpaid property taxes and demolished in 1996. (Courtesy of Charles H. Echols Jr.)

The "Oil Man," Thomas C. Driver of 227 Chestnut Street, was a busy oil distributor in Turner Station. In this October 5, 1957, picture he fills a 250-gallon oil tank for a customer in Day Village. Driver lived in the community since 1940. (Courtesy of the Afro-American Newspapers.)

Willie Marshall Sr. and his wife, Octavia, are shown in this photograph. They owned Marshall's Trash Removal, which they established in 1950. Octavia was very active in the business early on, driving the trucks alongside her husband. Marshall retired in 1987, turning the business over to his son. (Courtesy of the Marshall family.)

David Rice, shown here with his wife, Mary, started his trucking business in 1948. As an independent carrier, he transported loads along the East Coast for Bethlehem Steel as well as numerous other companies. Rice retired from the business in 1987. (Courtesy of the Rice family.)

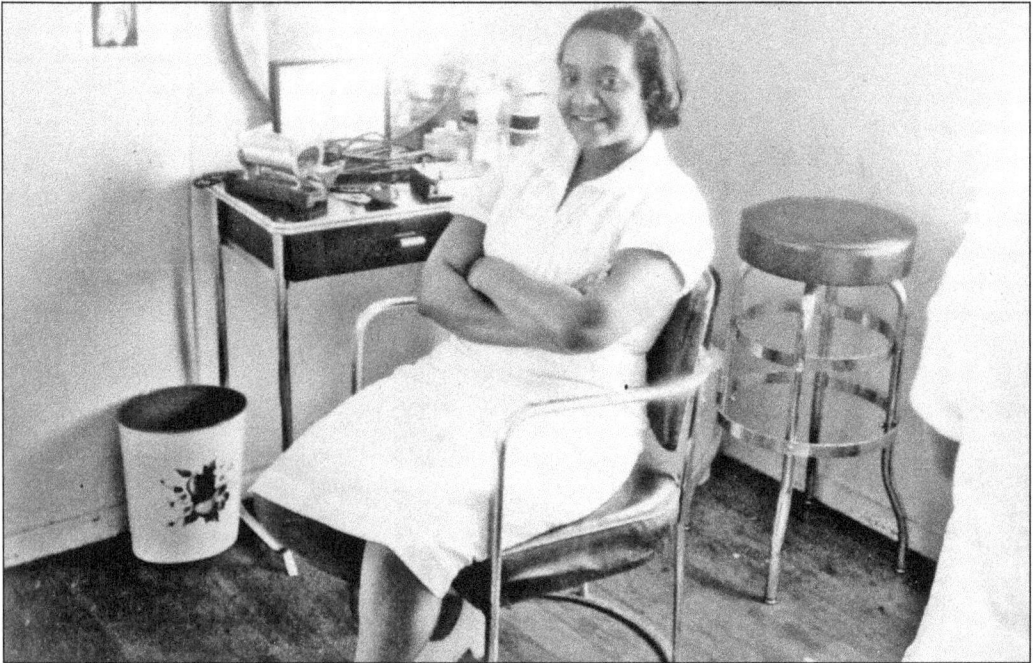

Vonzella Randolph was a local businesswoman. She is pictured above in her shop in the 1950s. Her business, the Cozy Corner Beauty Salon, was located on Sollers Point Road. (Courtesy of Vonzella Randolph.)

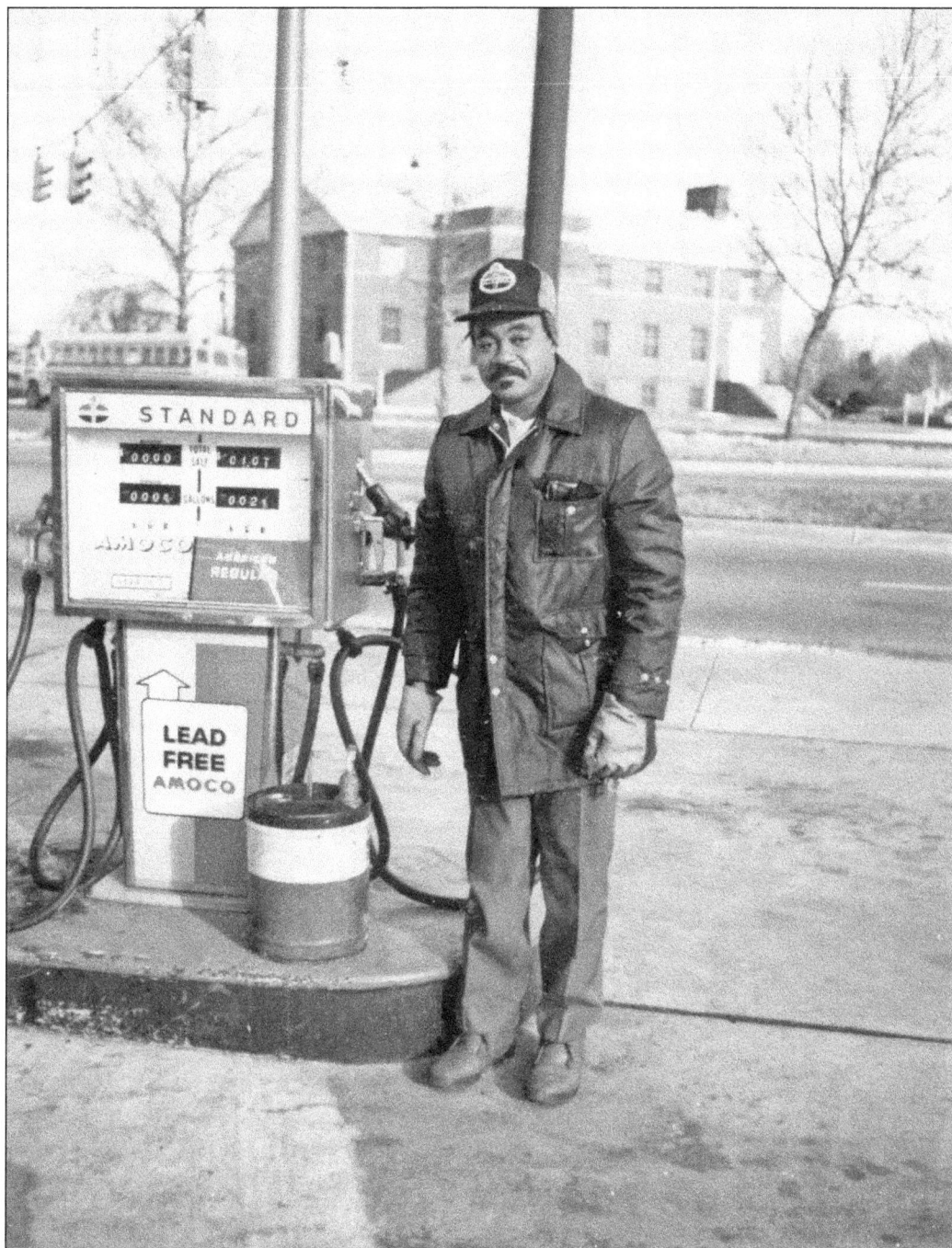

Mack Jones Sr. is seen at one of the pumps at the Jones Amoco gas station on Sollers Point Road in 1963. He and his brother, Eddie Jones, were owners and business partners in the station. (Courtesy of Mack Jones Sr.)

Wilson and Sons Grocery Store served residents of Sollers Homes in the 1940s and 1950s. In this 1950s photograph, a Schmidt Blue Ribbon Bread delivery truck is parked near the store. The business was located at 101 Blain Way and employed many people from the community. The Riverside Power Plant can be seen in the background. (Courtesy of the *Baltimore News-American*.)

This picture of a hog-killing was taken in 1941. At a time when Turner Station was mostly a wooded area with few homes, people recalled several areas where hogs were raised. Beatrice Curbeam, a resident of the community since 1935, indicated in an interview with Louis Diggs, "I remember the hog pens in the area where Day Village was built. I used to walk the kids down there, just to let them see all the hogs." (Courtesy of the Afro-American Newspapers.)

Six

RECREATION AND
ENTERTAINMENT

The Bobian Four are the children of Rev. King S. and Alice Bobian. Trained by their mother, Calvin started singing publicly at age two as part of his father's ministry. With the second son, Jay, they started singing duets. With Delores's voice, a trio was developed. When Shirley's voice was added, it resulted in their unique quartet harmony. They performed in churches, community affairs, county and state variety shows, and on radio and television. Pictured here in this 1960s photograph are, from left to right, Jay, Shirley, Delores, and Calvin Bobian. (Courtesy of Shirley Bobian Macklin.)

Members of the Turner Station Recreation Council meet at the Fleming Elementary School in this 1960s photograph. The recreation council was instrumental in promoting and supporting a variety of activities for the community's youth, including baseball, basketball, football, and the teen center. It is the oldest African American certified recreation council in Baltimore County, as it dates back to the late 1940s. (Courtesy of Charles and Veronica Mandy.)

Joseph Butler demonstrates his skills as a gymnast in this 1950s photograph. Butler worked for Bethlehem Steel from 1951 until his retirement in 1997. He was a shop steward, a union representative, and for four years was president of Local 2610, Steel Workers Union. He was also very active in the recreation council. (Courtesy of Joseph Butler.)

The Turner Station Hawks, a local baseball team, are seen above in 1958 at the Watersedge Ball Field. The team was followed enthusiastically by local residents and was sponsored by the late Dr. Joseph Thomas. (Courtesy of Maxine Waterhouse Thompson.)

Proud members of the Other Side of Town softball team display their trophies in this 1970s photograph. The team participated in a slow-pitch softball league and usually played their games at the ball field on the grounds of the former Fleming School. Edgar Toatley, the team manager, is standing on the left. (Courtesy of William and Verdella Minor.)

The Turner Station Recreation Council's annual opening-day parade launches the summer Little League baseball season in 1962. Members of the Turner Homes Dodgers baseball team proudly wear their uniforms and display their equipment. (Courtesy of the BCPL Legacy Web.)

Coaches and mentors Osceola Smith and Tileston Venable appear with one of the many teams they led as coaches in the Turner Station Recreation Council in the 1950s. The team members are, from left to right, (sitting on the grass) A. Ferguson; (first row) C. Winston, K. Lucas, S. Eppes, R. Wooten, J. Galloway, C. Smith, and W. Woods; (second row) M. Williams, I. Moore, D. Purvance, L. Sears, M. Ferguson, and D. Walls; (third row) D. Calloway, R. Gardner, C. Mercer, C. Batchelor, and W. Bruce; (last row) O. Smith, D. Alexander, and T. Venable. (Courtesy of the BCPL Legacy Web.)

Proud players from the 1964 Turner Station basketball team display their trophies. In the starting lineup are Sonny Banks (third from left), Carroll Evans (fourth from left), Meredith Smith (sixth from right), and M. Covington (third from right). Youth basketball was one of numerous sports sponsored and supported by the recreation council. (Courtesy of the BCPL Legacy Web.)

Members of the Turner Station men's baseball team are shown in this photograph from 1964. The players are, from left to right, as follows: (first row) J. Jones, G. Middleton, B. Seward, C. Wudtee, K. Solomon, P. Jones, and coach Pierce Jones Sr.; (second row) T. Williamson, J. Cromwell, C. Riddick, P. McGowan, B. Wynn, E. Wake, and H. Riddick; (third row) M. McGowan, R. Jones, J. Chambliss, P. Pack, L. Jeffers, and L. Wilson. (Courtesy of the BCPL Legacy Web.)

Quarterback Mike Pack is seen in this 1967 photograph with his coach, Robert Tamberella, just before the Baltimore County Championship game. Pack's team, the Dundalk Owls, was victorious over Sparrows Point High School 42-0. A multisport athlete who grew up in Turner Station, Pack was elected to the Greater Dundalk Sports Hall of Fame in 1990 and chosen "Citizen of the Year" for Greater Dundalk in 2007. (Courtesy of Mike Pack.)

Singer Pearl Bailey (below left, with Margaret Adams) was one of many well-known entertainers to perform at Adams Cocktail Lounge. The lounge attracted many of the true icons of the 1930s, 1940s, and 1950s, including Red Foxx, Billie Holiday, and big band leaders. Patrons from around the Baltimore area attended the club. The venue dwindled to a bar and package goods store in the 1970s and closed in 1986. (Courtesy of the BCPL Legacy Web.)

The Turner Station Recreation Council played a very instrumental and positive role in the development of the youth of the community. The organization's founding members are pictured above in the 1950s. They are, from left to right, James Hayes, Consuella Smith, David Barnett, Joseph Butler, Katherine Pounds, and Hiram Cleveland. (Courtesy of the BCPL Legacy Web.)

Myrtle Berman (left) and Nancy Taylor enjoy an evening out at Adams Bar and Cocktail Lounge. The ladies are in the Continental Room in this 1950 photograph at the popular local establishment in Turner Station. (Courtesy of Maxine Waterhouse Thompson.)

It's opening day at the beach, and young swimmers are eager and poised to enter the waters of Bear Creek. The Turner Station Recreation Council opened the Fleming Beach at Sollers Point for the enjoyment of the community, as seen in this 1964 photograph. (Courtesy of the BCPL Legacy Web.)

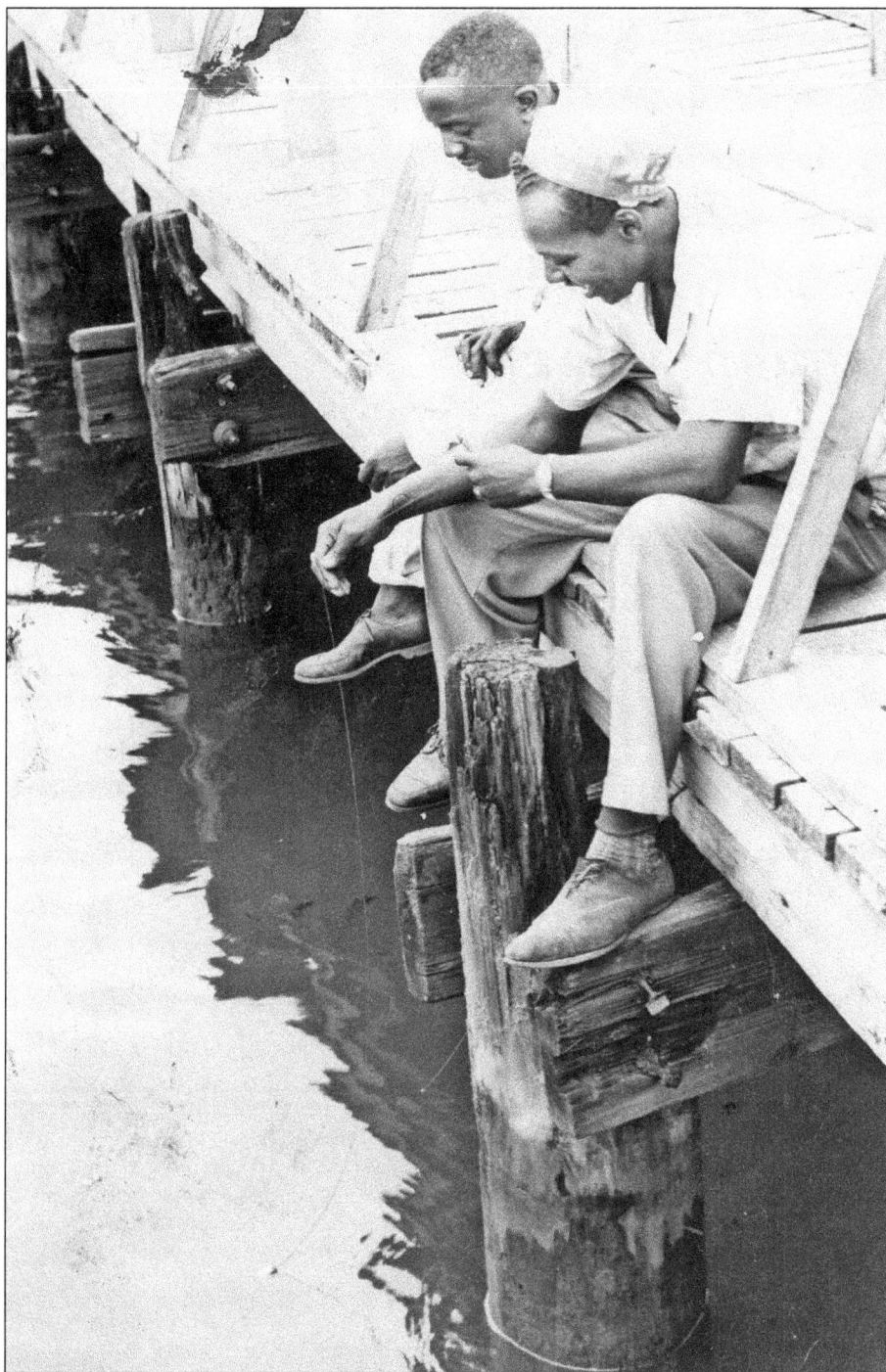

Fishing, crabbing, swimming, and boating were popular summer sports in the community of Turner Station, which is practically surrounded by water. From the smiles on the faces of Edward Alston (left) and James Lewis, Turner Station residents, it appeared that the crabs were biting from the pier at the foot of Avondale Road in Day Village on September 13, 1947. (Courtesy of the Afro-American Newspapers.)

This advertisement appeared June 4, 1932, in the Afro-American Newspapers. Dr. Thomas owned and operated Edgewater Beach (1929–1941), where he had a ball club and a large amusement park. Lots of people came from all over to enjoy the ball games, dancing, picnicking, swimming, boating and many other activities there. It was located on Sollers Point Road near the waterfront where the high school currently exists. (Courtesy of the Afro-American Newspapers.)

Seven

COMMUNITY
ORGANIZATIONS

This handsome group of young men strikes a classy pose in 1952. They called themselves the Dukes Club, a self-organized social club of young men in Turner Station. (Courtesy of the BCPL Legacy Web.)

These beautiful young ladies attended the Tri Hi Y Debutante Ball at Sollers Point High School in 1950. The affair was sponsored by the Turner Station YMCA. Members included here are M. Harris, G. Tyler, H. Henderson, R. Jones, D. Potee, C. Merritt, C. Fawcett, B. Gilmore (leader), M. Barnett, E. Evans, N. Robinson, S. Logan, and A. Williamson. (Courtesy of Elsie Winston.)

Members of Boy Scout Troop No. 270 pose for this 1950s unit photograph during an encampment at Broad Creek, Maryland. Scoutmaster James Louden is in the back. The unit participated in this annual camping trip with many similar units from around the state. Louden was an active leader of the community's recreation council, in addition to serving for decades as a Boy Scout leader. (Courtesy of the Louden family.)

Citizens of Turner Station served and supported their community as members of the Turner Station Auxiliary Police Detachment. Officers on the 1958 roster are shown above. Working in conjunction with officers from the Dundalk police barracks, they provided local security and were the first black unit in Baltimore County. (Courtesy of the Louden family.)

The Brown Buddies was a Social Club originally founded around 1948 by members of the Union Baptist Church in Sparrows Point, Maryland. The individuals in this 1948 photograph are (left to right) Nellie Glenn, Vernell Poole, Agnes Fowlkes, Anna Ruth Cheatham, two unidentified, Marion Cole, Augusta Bullett, Ann Tilghman, Ruth Lewis, and Jimmy Brown. Their activities included holding fund-raisers to benefit the church and the community. (Courtesy of Jacqueline Knight.)

Residents of Turner Station successfully raised $10,000 to purchase the community center building. Shown in this 1948 photograph are, from left to right, William C. Darden, D. Byrd, Dr. Arthur L. Johnson (chairman of the drive), Henry A. Brook, Avon B. Collins, and Dr. William C. Wade. Plans were made to have childcare, health care, and recreational activities in the building in the future. (Courtesy of the Afro-American Newspapers.)

This building served as the community center for various activities, the library, and the YMCA. Its principal function was that of a library. The Turner Station Library was originally housed at 407 North Avondale Road in Day Village. It was the product of the vision and efforts of Elizabeth McDaniel and Maeives Addison, two local educators. In 1948, it came under the Baltimore County Public Library System and moved to a permanent site in the old community building above at 411 New Pittsburg Avenue. The library closed and was merged with the North Point branch in 1993. (Courtesy of the BCPL Legacy Web.)

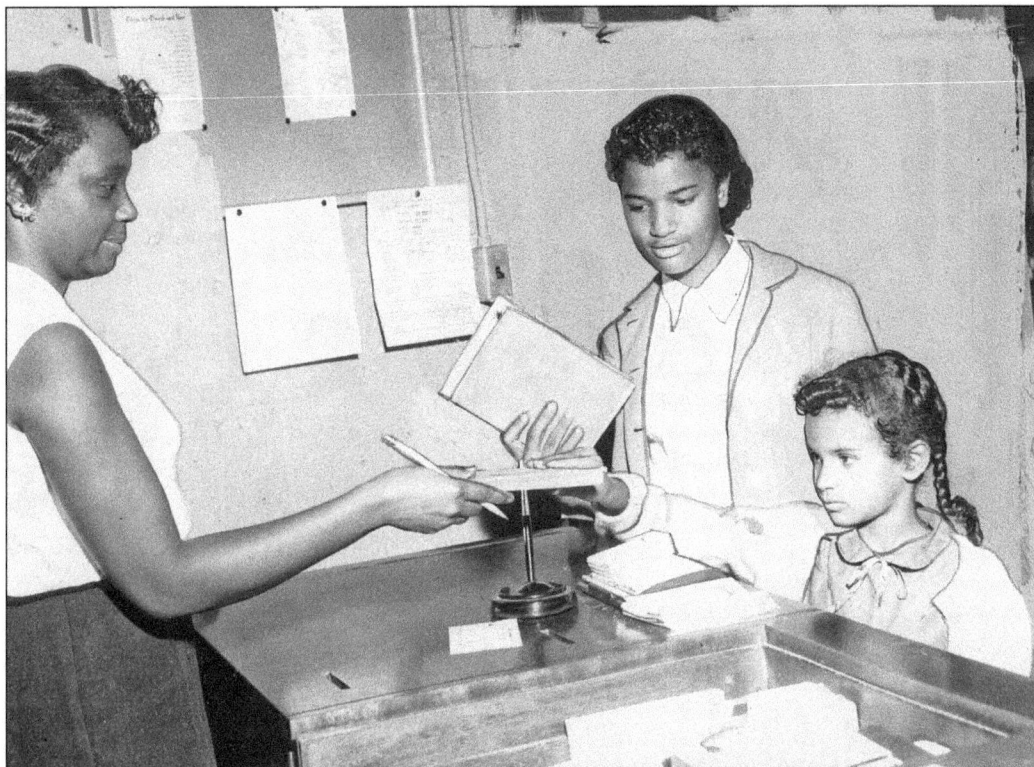

Maeives Addison, librarian at the Baltimore County Library in Turner Station, issues a book to six-year-old Rosalind Oliver, daughter of Robert and Marguerite Oliver. On the right in this October 1957 photograph is Veronica Oliver, 14, sister of Rosalind. (Courtesy of the Afro-American Newspapers.)

David Stinson and Adelle Lacy take full advantage of the offerings at the library in the community center building in this 1957 photograph. The two are students of Fleming Elementary School but attend classes in the community center building. The well-equipped library is part of the Baltimore County Public Library System. (Courtesy of the Afro-American Newspapers.)

Twenty-five members of the Turner Station Speech Choir perform at the Community Center in this 1954 photograph. Members are, from left to right, (first row), unidentified, James Bobian, Yvonne Wilbourne, Alice Mason, Gloria Mason-Lewis, unidentified, Deanna Barnett, James Johnson, and unidentified; (second row) unidentified, Sonya Turnipseed, three unidentified, Sylvia Williams, Flavia Williams, unidentified, and Calvin Bobian. All in the third row are unidentified except Arnedia Brown (far right). (Courtesy of Shirley Bobian Macklin.)

The Veterans of Foreign Wars Post No. 4438 received their charter in November 1966. There were 40 charter members. The post was located at 411-A New Pittsburg Avenue in Turner Station. In December 1981, post commander Roscoe Burman negotiated with the Turner Station Progressive Association, Inc., to make the VFW the trustees of the community center building. The VFW's mission is to "honor the dead by helping the living." (Courtesy of the Afro-American Newspapers.)

Members of the Turner Station Youth Committee meet in May 1965 in the office of Dr. Theodore Patterson. The group planned a luncheon to launch a new program that targeted the community's youth. The program encouraged young people to become involved in more constructive activities. Committee members are, from left to right, Dr. Theodore Patterson, Lucille Wade, Mildred Williams, and Johnson McClurkin. (Courtesy of the Afro-American Newspapers.)

Polio shots are administered to this group of Turner Station residents in the temporary health clinic offices in Sollers Homes in April 1958. The charge nurse, Agnes Williams, speaks to the group as the second nurse, Evelyn Moran, fills out the paperwork. The United States experienced an outbreak of 58,000 and 35,000 polio cases in 1952 and 1953, up from a typical number of around 20,000 cases a year. The community had a campaign to build a new health center. (Courtesy of the Afro-American Newspapers.)

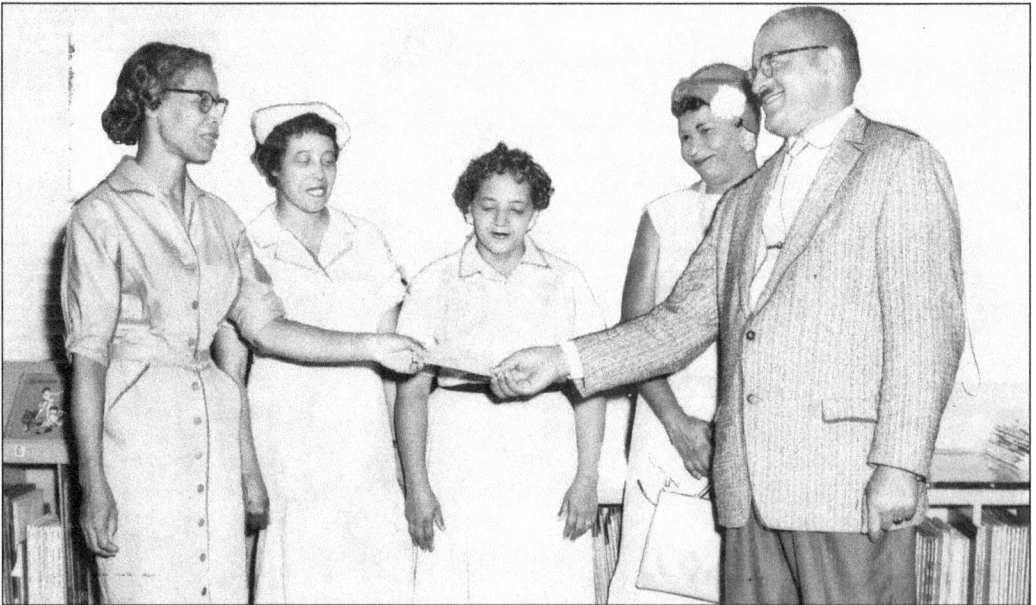

On June 24, 1958, Turner Station Health Committee's building fund was the recipient of a donation by the Fleming School PTA. Mary E. Harris, left, principal of Fleming Elementary School, turns a check over to Robert Lee Abbott, president of the committee. Looking on from left to right are public health nurse Agnes Williams, and committee members Doris Waddell and Maude Vaughn. (Courtesy of the Afro-American Newspapers.)

Turner Station's new health center was bought with donations from the residents of Turner Station and private contributions. This duplex building located in Lyon Homes at 11-13 South Lane was renovated and converted into a health center. The center opened in February 1961. (Courtesy of the Afro-American Newspapers.)

More than 200 people from the community visited the Turner Station Health Center's open house on April 24, 1961. Standing in front of the building are members of the Turner Health Committee and representatives from donating organizations. The two walkers and wheelchair were donated by the Northern Central District of the American Legion Womens' Auxiliary. (Courtesy of the Afro-American Newspapers.)

Eight

PEOPLE TO REMEMBER

Dr. Joseph Thomas, seen above in his medical office, was a physician, businessman, and diplomat. Born in 1884, he opened the community's first medical practice in 1918. He was the area's first postmaster, opened the first black-owned housing development—the 12-unit Anthony Homes—and operated the Anthony Theater. He was also owner of the Edgewater Beach and a Negro League baseball team, the Baltimore Grays. Dr. Thomas passed away in 1963. (Courtesy of Charles H. Echols.)

Dr. Joseph Thomas and his wife, Flavia (second from left), attended this reception in the home of Dr. and Mrs. Ernest Haydel in New Orleans, Louisiana. With the Thomases are C. C. Haydel and his wife, Dana. (Courtesy of Dr. Theodore C. Patterson.)

Dr. Thomas' yacht, *Fla-Joe*, was an 83-foot surplus air-sea rescue vessel purchased for about $3,000 from the U.S. Coast Guard. The boat saw action during World War II. Dr. Thomas made extensive repairs and renovations so that the boat's value in the 1950s was estimated at $100, 000. *Fla-Joe* provided countless hours of enjoyment at sea along the Chesapeake and the East Coast for Dr. Thomas, his family, and friends. (Courtesy of the BCPL Legacy Web.)

This aerial photograph, taken sometime in the 1930s, shows the property of Dr. Joseph Thomas and his wife, Flavia. They owned 475 acres of land in Edgewater. His home, with a boat docked in the pier, is in the left foreground. Their property extended over to Turner Station, which is located south of the intersection of Dundalk Avenue and Sollers Point Road on the upper left. (Courtesy of Charles H. Echols.

J. Bruce Turner is seen in this 1950s photograph. Turner was a physical education teacher and track coach at Sollers Point High School from 1948 to 1957. He started a successful track program at the school and built its first track, which was later named in his honor. (Courtesy of the Afro-American Newspapers.)

Maeives Addison receives a well-deserved service award at the BCPL annual meeting in October 1981. A longtime resident of Turner Station, Addison was the community's first librarian in 1943. She continued in that role with the move of the library to the old community building on New Pittsburg Avenue. The library became part of the Baltimore County Public Library system in 1948. (Courtesy of the BCPL Legacy Web.)

Henrietta Lacks, seen here with her husband, was diagnosed with cervical cancer at Johns Hopkins Hospital in February 1951. The Turner Station resident died of that disease in October that year. Her blood cells (later called "HeLa" cells) were able to reproduce themselves outside of the body. These unique cells were used in numerous medical experiments all over the world. In 1954, Dr. Jonas Salk worked with her cells in developing the polio vaccine. (Courtesy of the BCPL Legacy Web.)

Dr. William C. Wade, a general practitioner, presents certificates of academic achievement to this group of students from Sollers Point High School in the 1960s. Dr. Wade came to Turner Station in 1944. He practiced medicine from his office at 138–140 Oak Avenue, and served the community until his retirement in the 1980s. (Courtesy of Linda Lucille Wade Hurd.)

The Turner Station community has always been supportive of its schools. In the above photograph, taken in the 1950s, a group of PTA members are shown at the Turner Elementary School. Pictured are Robert Abbott (seated) and, from left to right, A. Eley, H. Speaks, M. Abbott, V. Devine, M. Wilson, Eliza McDaniel, and D. Waddell. Abbott was often referred to as the "Mayor of Turner Station" by virtue of his involvement and active leadership in many aspects of the community's affairs. (Courtesy of the BCPL Legacy Web.)

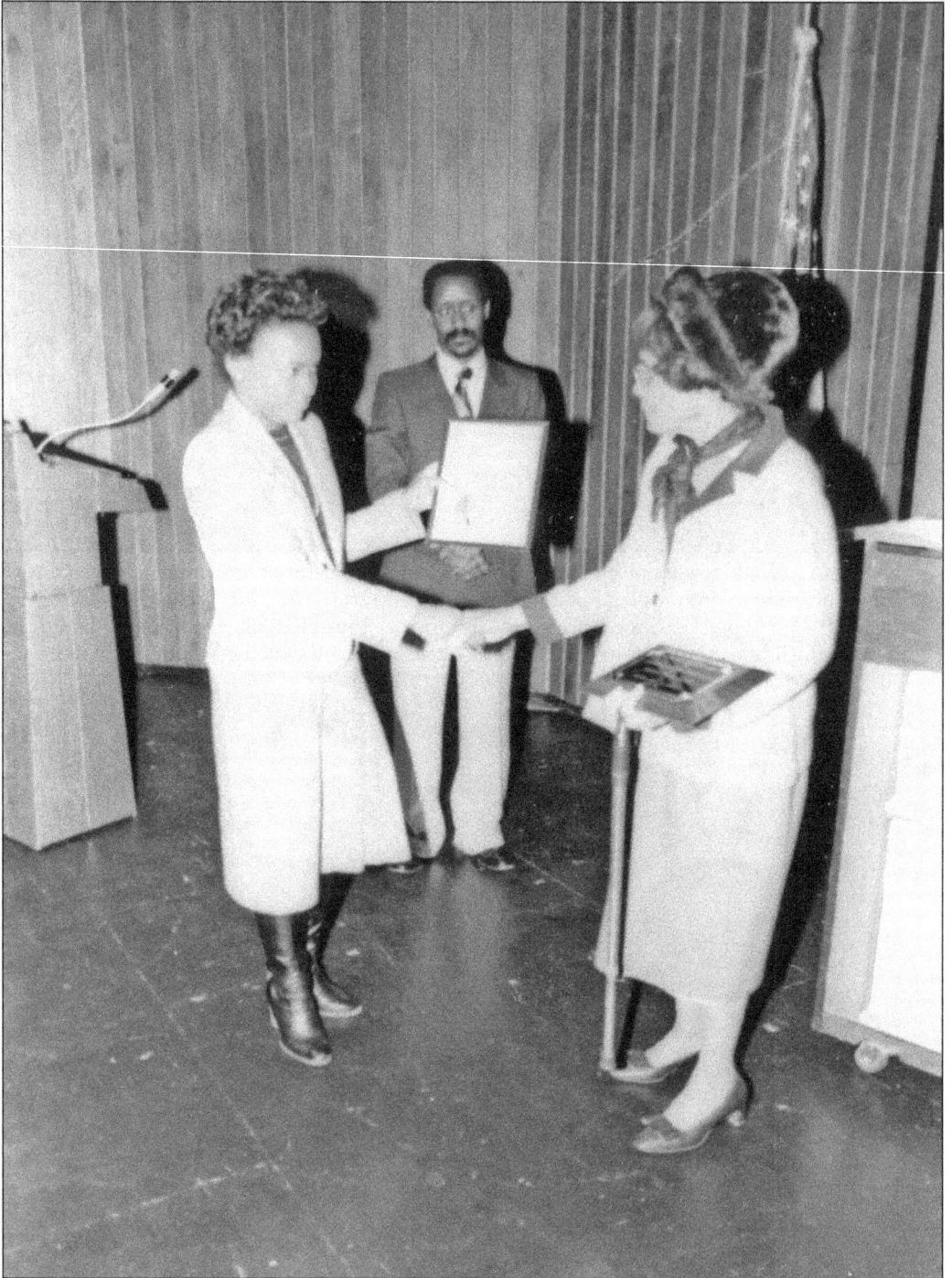

Eliza S. McDaniels (right) is given a Community Service Award during a 1980s Black History Month program at the Dundalk Community College. McDaniels was instrumental in the creation of the community's first library in the 1940s. She was a teacher and pupil personnel worker for many years in Baltimore County. Presenting the award is Adrienne Jones, an aide to the Baltimore County executive. (Courtesy of Dunbar Brooks.)

Louis and Elsie Winston appear in this formal 1960 portrait. Elsie was quite active in the recreation council for many years. She was a leader/coach in the girls' softball and basketball programs. Louis was a member of the outstanding foursome that won the mile relay title at the Penn Relays in the 1950s. (Courtesy of the BCPL Legacy Web.)

Osceola and Consuella Smith are shown at left in 1982. Smith, or "Smitty" as he was known, was a local legend in the community. He also played semi-professional baseball in the 1930s with great Negro League players such as Satchel Paige and Josh Gibson. His contributions to the youth of Turner Station were significant. As a coach and mentor in baseball, basketball, and football, he touched the lives of hundreds of young people. He was inducted into the Greater Dundalk Sports Hall of Fame in 1984. (Courtesy of Mary Livingston.)

Dr. Theodore C. Patterson, shown in this 1979 photograph, was a member of the first graduating class of Sollers Point High School in 1949. Born and raised in Sparrows Point, Dr. Patterson joined Dr. Joseph Thomas in his practice in 1962 after completing medical school. With the passing of Dr. Thomas in 1963, he took over the practice, serving both the Dundalk and Turner Station communities until retiring in 1992. (Courtesy of Dr. Theodore C. Patterson.)

This popular singing group, the Calvin Statham Singers, celebrates its 45th anniversary in April 1995. Malvin Patrick Statham is standing by his father, Calvin Statham, Sparrows Point native and founder/leader of the group. Standing, from left to right, are Lyndale Weaver, Malvilyn Statham, Delores Gregory, and Annie Trent (of Turner Station). Calvin and Malvilyn were married at the Union Baptist Church in 1964. Malvilyn was a member of the legendary gospel group the Clara Ward singers. (Courtesy of Calvin and Malvilyn Statham.)

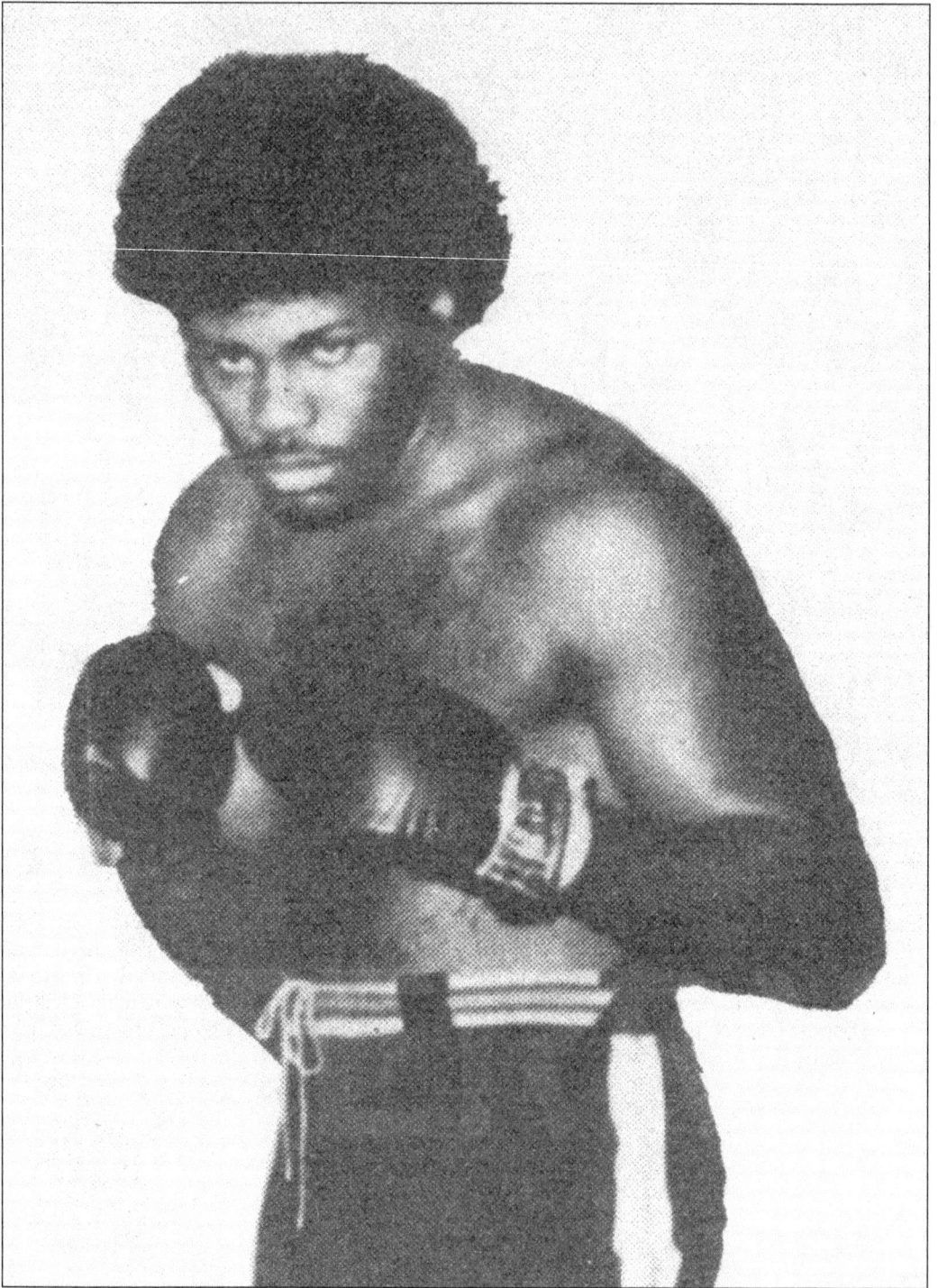

Larry Middleton (above) was a world-ranked heavyweight boxer. His career extended from 1965 to 1976. During that time, he fought a variety of ranked contenders. Among his notable opponents were Ken Norton (a former champion), Ron Lyle, Jimmy Ellis (a former champion), Oscar Bonavena, Joe Bugner, and Jerry Quarry. (Courtesy of Larry Middleton.)

120

Former resident Calvin Hill (right) is shown with Osceola Smith (center) of the Turner Station Recreation Council and Bob Staab of Baltimore County Recreation and Parks during an Award Night activity around 1970. Hill, a Yale University graduate, was drafted by the Dallas Cowboys in 1969. In addition to Dallas, the star running back played for the Washington Redskins and the Cleveland Browns during a 12-year NFL career. He was chosen All-Pro on four different occasions. (Courtesy of the BCPL Legacy Web.)

Local members of the Dundalk–Sparrows Point Branch of the NAACP protest against an anti-busing amendment before Congress in August 1979. The demonstration took place in Washington, D.C., and included, from left to right, Ora Coles, Jean Coles, Martha Hunt, Dunbar Brooks (president), and Catherine Pounds from Turner Station. (Courtesy of Dunbar Brooks.)

Kweisi Mfume (standing, left) appeared in a parade in support of the Turner Station Recreation Council in this 1964 photograph. He spent his formative years in Turner Station. His political career began with the Baltimore City Council, where he served from 1979 to 1986. He ran successfully for the U.S. Congress from the Seventh Congressional District, serving from 1986 to 1995. While in congress, Mfume led the Congressional Black Caucus (1992–1994). In 1995, he resigned from the House of Representatives and was chosen to be president and chief executive officer of the NAACP (1995–2005). (Courtesy of the BCAL Legacy Web.)

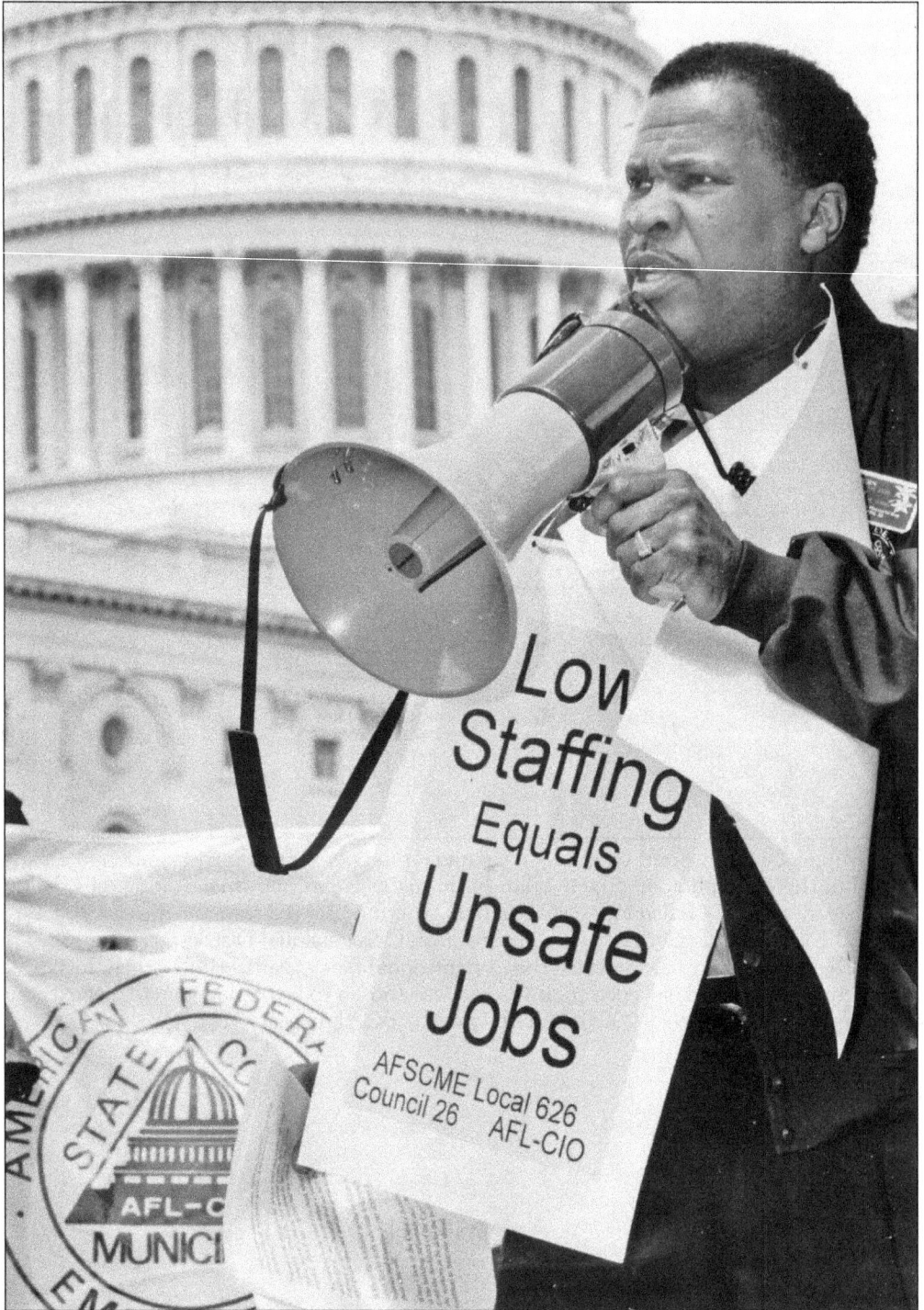

Glenard S. Middleton, a longtime labor union activist, is shown above in 2006. He is president of AFSCME Local 44, a labor organization representing 1,300 school custodians. Middleton is also vice president of the Maryland–D.C. AFL-CIO. He was born and raised in Turner Station and is the brother of boxer Larry Middleton. (Courtesy of Glenard Middleton.)

Astronaut Robert Curbeam (standing on left) is seen above in his NASA space gear with other members of the crew for his first shuttle mission. The Naval Academy graduate served as a mission specialist on a six-person crew on the space shuttle mission STS-85 in August 1997. He also participated in a second mission in 2001. He retired from the navy in 2007. (Courtesy of Mary Livingston.)

George (left), Anita (center), and Kevin Clash are shown in 1964. The youngest of the trio, Kevin, has become a nationally known puppeteer. He is the voice of Elmo the Muppet on the children's television program *Sesame Street*. (Courtesy of the BCPL Legacy Web.)

This is a photograph of two-year-old Kevin Clash between three of his puppet characters, which he drew when he was about 10 years old. His artistic and creative talents were apparent at an early age. (Courtesy of the Clash family.)

Turner Station's pride and joy, Kevin Clash, appears with his parents, George and Gladys Clash, at the Turner Station Heritage Foundation's Where's Elmo? event on the Community College of Baltimore County–Dundalk campus on October 14, 2000. Kevin was born and raised in Turner Station. (Courtesy of the Clash family.)

BIBLIOGRAPHY

The Baltimore *Afro-American*. Baltimore, MD: October 5, 1957.

Cozzens, Lisa. "Early Civil Rights Struggles: *Brown v. Board of Education*." 2002. www.watson. org/Lisa/blackhistory/earlycivilrights/brown.

Diggs, Louis S. *From the Meadows to the Point*. Baltimore: Uptown Press, 2003.

Dundalk: The First Hundred Years 1895–1995. Dundalk, MD: Dundalk–Patapsco Neck Historical Society, 1997.

Hall, Elmer J. *Diary of A Mill Town: Recollections of the Bungalows and Sparrows Point, Maryland*. Indiana, PA: Halldin Publishing, 2003.

Harwood, Herbert H. *Baltimore and Its Streetcars*. New York: Quadrant Press, 1984.

"The Little Town that Could." *The Dundalk Eagle*. Dundalk, MD: July 2002.

McGrain, John. Baltimore County Historian to Dave Albright (Internal Correspondence). March 11, 1982.

McGrain, John. Letter to the author. 2002.

Patterson, Theodore C. "The Educational Journey of African-Americans in Southeastern Baltimore County." Unpublished paper, 1999.

The *Sunday Sun*. Baltimore, MD: June 4, 1978.

Watson, Jerome R. *Remembering Our Schools*. Baltimore: Uptown Press, 2004.

———. *The Churches of Turner Station*. Baltimore: Uptown Press, 2002.

Visit us at
arcadiapublishing.com

www.ingramcontent.com/pod-product-compliance
Lightning Source LLC
Chambersburg PA
CBHW050704150426
42813CB00055B/2453